LOST IN WONDER

LOST IN WONDER

Charles Wesley

THE MEANING OF HIS HYMNS TODAY

S T Kimbrough, Jr.

The Upper Room
Nashville, Tennessee

Lost in Wonder

The cover illustration is adapted from an engraving which is part of the collection of the John Street United Methodist Church, New York City.

Book and Cover Design: Steve Laughbaum
First Printing: May, 1987(7)
Library of Congress Catalog Card Number: 86-051154
ISBN 0-8358-0558-1

Printed in the United States of America

To my mother and father,
Dorothy and S T, who first sang to me
the hymns of Charles Wesley

Contents

Each question is accompanied by the first line of a Wesley hymn/poem to which it refers. Those marked with an asterisk (*) are not printed in entirety.

III Faith

IV Others and the World

V Ourselves

VI Daily Living

Foreword

Charles Wesley, one of the world's most beloved hymn writers, never composed a piece of music, so far as we know. Although the mention of "O for a Thousand Tongues to Sing" or "Hark! The Herald-Angels Sing" or "A Charge to Keep I Have" elicits the memory of familiar tunes, it is the words, not the music, that give these hymns their power. With all due respect to the many composers (from Carl von Weber to Felix Mendelssohn-Bartholdy to Lowell Mason) who gave melodies to Charles's poetry, we recognize that the lasting grasp on our hearts and minds comes from what Shakespeare called "the force of a heaven-bred poesy."

Poetry is perhaps the most appropriate form for a theology of the heart; the words often communicate to the soul even before they are understood by the mind. The power of Wesley's poetry is its evocative nature—the words call forth images that are immediately sensible and personally relevant. Wesley's poetry is conceived within a vibrant sense of the divine-human relationship, and from the experience of this reality emerge words and images that convey the depth and breadth of Christian experience. The vigor and intensity of his own experience is transmitted in images that speak with clarity and power and in a form that transcends the pedantic tendencies of prose theology. Charles has mastered the art of poetic expression by marshalling verbal symbols that give perceptive form to the palpitations of his heart.

His brother John felt that Charles's poetry unfolded "the purity, the strength, and the elegance of the English language" as well as "the true spirit of poetry." But the practical impact of his work was even more easily definable. Charles's hymns came to represent the popular form of Wesleyan theology; the eighteenth-century revival was to a great extent borne on the wings of Charles's poetry. Charles's hymns not only helped form the texture of the Methodist mind but also, perhaps more importantly, set the temper of the Methodist spirit.

The language of Wesley's poetry is biblical and personal; the images have vigor and intensity. While some of the hymns have been sung in public worship for generations, others of the poems were written intentionally for private use. Both are works of devotional art and can appropriately be incorporated into private devotion and meditation.

From the vast depository of Wesleyan poetry, not all of it equally masterful, S T Kimbrough, Jr. has here chosen some of the best examples of Charles's hymns and poems that continue to speak to our own conditions and situations. His selection further illustrates John Telford's comment on Charles that "every side of life stirred his muse." These poems and the commentary upon them are more than meditations upon personal experience; they exhibit and examine many of the basic questions of human existence. With prayerful use, the reader can not only expect to wrestle with the "Traveller unknown," but can also hope to share the joy of a life "lost in wonder, love, and praise."

RICHARD P. HEITZENRATER
Southern Methodist University
Dallas, Texas

(*) Daddy's favorite hymn

Preface

This book begins with "Come, O thou Traveller unknown," of which Isaac Watts said, "That single poem, 'Wrestling Jacob,' is worth all the verses I myself have written." It is Charles Wesley's spiritual autobiography and summarizes his life, work, and ministry. It raises the question he is ever asking:

> Wilt thou not yet to me reveal
> Thy new unutterable name?

In his hymns and poems, Charles Wesley takes all who sing and read on a journey inward, asking soul-searching questions which are as up-to-date now as they were in the eighteenth century. They reflect his quest for identity as a human being, clergyman, and follower of Jesus Christ. His questions about God, Jesus, faith, others and the world, self, and daily living are today's questions. This book is not an exhaustive study of such questions or another analysis of Wesleyan history, theology, or hymnody. It is simply an attempt to look afresh at questions we are asking which are contained in familiar and unfamiliar hymns and poems of Charles Wesley.

In some instances, more stanzas are included than will be found in most hymnbooks, especially where they enhance understanding. However, no attempt has been made to print every poem in its entirety. Where stanzas have been omitted, the first line of the poem, as listed in the Contents, is marked with an asterisk. The stanzas as printed here often are designated in the discussions by number, such as, stanza one or two. This is for clarity in reference to the order in which they appear on the printed pages of this book and does not necessarily indicate Wesley's own sequence of the stanzas. Following the last line of each poem, the title of its original source appears.

Widely accepted revised forms of some hymns as they appear in many hymnbooks are often used. Occasionally, however, an original wording has been restored where the revised form has greatly changed Wesley's original intention. While Wesley lived in a time which did not express the kind of concern for inclusive language voiced today, he used much language which is quite compatible with that concern, such as, "Parent of Good" as a form of divine address and occasionally "human kind" instead of "mankind" (see his *Hymns for the Use of Families,* 1767). Very little has been done to adjust the language of many of his hymns which have become a part of the "memory bank" of English-speaking Christendom. In some instances, inclusive language changes which do not affect rhyme, assonance, and alliteration have been made, as well as a few for clarity and contemporary relevance. On the whole, the attempt has been made to be faithful to Wesley's texts as written. They possess an integrity on their own as theology, literature, and art. At the conclusion of the book there is a list of original lines which I have revised. Such revisions have been made from the viewpoint of hymns as living worship or liturgy and not as dead, verbal relics of the past, and by utilizing Wesley's own vocabulary. In utilizing the traditional language in Wesley's hymns and poems today, it is paramount to remember the overarching pluralistic, inclusive, and universalistic spirit of his theology.

The Charles Wesley poetry is the largest lyrical commentary on the Christian faith, life, and the scriptures to be found in the English language. About 9,000 hymns and poems may be attributed to him. While hundreds of them were written as hymns, many were never intended to be sung. His primary sources were the King James Version of the Bible, the Book of Common Prayer, the early fathers of the church, numerous poets of his day, and the God and people whom he served. Unfortunately, over the years the bulk of Wesley's poetry has become increasingly inaccessible to the church at large, as has that of other poets in his family: father Samuel, brothers John and Samuel, and sister Mehetabel.

A primary reason for this book is to make a broader range of Wesley's works available to the general public, and I am deeply grateful to the Center of Theological Inquiry, its chancellor, Dr. James I. McCord, and staff for support and assistance during the writing of the book. I am also indebted to Dr. Frank Baker and Dr. Oliver Beckerlegge for invaluable historical and textual insight, as well as accessibility to unpublished work of Charles Wesley, and to Dr. Richard Heitzenrater for his interest and Foreword to the volume.

The hymns and poems included here take us on an inner spiritual journey of growth in faith. This is why they were written. Many of them will gain a signficance they have lost when we see them anew or for the first time in relation to history, theology, tradition, the church, the Wesleys, life today, and ourselves.

S T Kimbrough, Jr.
Center of Theological Inquiry
Princeton, New Jersey

Introduction

Charles Wesley is unquestionably one of Christendom's greatest poets. Many of the approximately 9,000 poems he wrote during his lifetime have been set to music for use as hymns. They may be found in almost every English language Christian hymnal regardless of denomination. Wesley was a master of words and was steeped in a strong classical educational tradition which gave him facility in Latin and biblical languages, and a firm foundation in history, theology, and literature. Charles's father, Samuel, a village Anglican clergyman and an astute classical scholar, and his mother, Susanna, a master of children's education, provided the solid classical training in the home during their children's early years.

Charles came by his poetical gifts rightly, as his father, two brothers, Samuel and John, and a sister Mehetabel, published poetry. Another thing which the three brothers shared in common was ordination as clergymen of the Church of England.

At eight years of age Charles left home to attend Westminster School and later entered Christ Church College of Oxford where he received the B.A. and M.A. degrees. It was there that his poetical prowess began to develop as he transcribed, translated, and paraphrased many of the great classical poets, especially the Latin ones. Simultaneously, his interest in spiritual growth was developing. Charles's poetical and spiritual interests were destined to be wedded throughout his life.

During his third or fourth year at Oxford, Charles and his brother John formed a small group of students who were later called "Methodists" because of their methodical concern for the daily routine of living a holy life. They were committed to study, prayer, social service, and weekly attendance at Holy Communion. A lifelong partnership in the journey of faith and ministry began for Charles and John. They went to America as missionaries in 1735 on the same ship, their conversion experiences in 1738 took place in London during the same week, they traveled and preached side by side, they sang, prayed, and worshiped together, they co-edited and published hymnbooks and *Notes on the New Testament,* they were persecuted often by the same violent mobs, they laughed and cried together, and they shared many of their deepest thoughts with each other. Unfortunately, because of their close identity, the uniqueness of Charles's individual creativity, thought, and contributions often has been lost. He has stood much too long in John's shadow. To be sure, John was the organizer, leader, systematic thinker, writer, and publisher and Charles was the troubadour, bard, poet. However, Charles was no less a systematic thinker or effective preacher and theologian than John; but he did couch his thought in the mystery and eloquence of poetical language which could not always be subjected to the closely-reasoned argument so characteristic of John's writing.

Charles proceeded systematically through the Bible and wrote poetry on numerous passages from almost all its books. The two volumes, *Short Hymns on Select Passages of the Holy Scriptures* (1762), remain one of the richest lyrical commentaries on the Bible in the English language.

Indeed, Charles and John were much alike in doctrine and faith perspective. Both were evangelical and sacramental Christians who sought a fervent inner encounter with God through Christ and a strong practice of living worship centered in regular Holy Communion, preaching, daily prayers, and whatever good they might do for the bodies and souls of all whom they encountered.

Nevertheless, Charles was very different from John. He was a modest man and consumed with a passion to communicate the Christian faith and to capture its wonder and mystery in the language of poetry. Rarely a day passed without his writing lyrics. John was also an excellent poet, as his translations of over thirty German hymns reflect. But he was more involved in organizing the distribution of Charles's poetry than in writing his own. We can find many clues to differences in their thinking in the stanzas of hymns and poems John often omitted and/or changed when he edited Charles's works for publication. He sometimes found Charles's lyrics too sentimental or mystical and occasionally theologically misleading. Charles ardently opposed John on the separation of the Methodist societies from the Church of England and the ordination of American "Methodist" bishops. He also spelled out in the 1762 volumes mentioned previously his views on gradual sanctification which were by no means in every point synonymous with John's.

John has often been designated the preacher-organizer-theologian and Charles the poet-artist-theologian. More simply put, some would say John was the preacher and Charles was the singer. Charles, however, was also a forceful preacher and spent much time and energy for the improvement of preaching. One of the most widely distributed Methodist pamphlets during the second half of the eighteenth century was his sermon, "Awake, Thou that Sleepest!" first delivered in 1742 at Oxford. John was certainly a more prolific writer of prose than Charles and his contributions to Christian theology and religious awakening are monumental. By comparison, however, many more people around the world today sing Charles's hymns than read John's theology. This has more to do with the nature of the hymns than with John's theology. Charles's poetry transcends the idiosyncrasies of denominations and points directly to the inward witness of God's Spirit in human lives.

Many of Wesley's poems were born out of conflict, crisis, violence, oppression, and opposition, and are still timely today. They have spread around the world wherever people suffer, rejoice, and worship, for their message of self-giving love, as Wesley experienced it in Christ, redeems the time and those who sing them. The questions he was asking all his life are the questions we are asking today. Therefore, we see our lives mirrored in his words. The questions may take other forms, be expanded or altered, but the basic questions are the same because they have to do with what life ultimately means.

My aim has been to take a fresh look at the unique way in which Charles Wesley asked in the eighteenth century questions which are still primary today. This is something he did by way of poetry, which is distinctively different from John. In these pages he is seen as evangelist, churchman, and poet through history, theology and life today.

At his conversion Charles wrote a hymn which asks the question: "Where shall my wondering soul begin?" His boldness to ask himself that question in the face of commitment is a valuable guide for discipleship and life's pilgrimage as a follower of Jesus. We must always be bold to inquire and question. Wesley helps us do that. Above all, he helps us ask ourselves the questions that matter most.

A Charles Wesley Time Line

1707	Dec. 18	born at Epworth
1709	Feb. 9	rescued from Epworth Rectory fire
1716		enters Westminster School
1726		enters Christ Church College, Oxford
1730		receives B.A. degree, becomes tutor at Oxford
1733		receives M.A. degree
1735	Apr. 25	father Samuel dies
	Sept. 21	ordained deacon of the Church of England by Dr. John Potter, Bishop of Oxford
	Sept. 24	appointed secretary for Indian Affairs, American colony of Georgia
	Sept. 29	ordained priest of the Church of England by Dr. Edmund Gibson, Bishop of London
	Oct. 14	Charles and John embark at Gravesend on the ship Simmonds for Georgia; during the voyage they encounter on board the Moravians' deep Christian faith and singing
1736	Feb. 5	lands in Savannah
	March	proceeds to Frederica where he takes up his minstry
	March 9	begins his published *Journal*
	July 26	leaves Georgia overland for Charleston where he embarks for England; becomes severely ill on board and ship lands for a time in Boston
	Dec. 3	lands in Deal, England and proceeds to London
1737		meets Moravian leader, Count Zinzendorf, in London

1738		meets Moravian Peter Böhler whom he begins teaching English
	Apr. 3	resigns his Georgia secretaryship
	May 21	Charles Wesley experiences "conversion"
	May 24	John Wesley experiences "conversion"
1739		begins major publications of hymns/poems with John: *Hymns and Sacred Poems;* first Methodist house of worship is established: "New Room" at Bristol
	May 29	preaches in fields for first time
	Nov. 6	brother Samuel dies
1742		preaches in the north of England with brother John for first time; they establish their first orphanage and Sunday School
	July 23	mother Susanna dies
1744		first Methodist Conference at the Foundry; Methodist districts are established throughout England
1747	Sept. 9-March 20, 1748	visits Ireland for first time
1748	Aug. 13-Oct. 8	visits Ireland for second time
1749		publishes *Hymns and Sacred Poems*
	Apr. 8	marries Sarah Gwynne; officiant is brother John
	Sept. 1	acquires house in Charles Street, Bristol
1752	Aug.	son John Wesley is born (Note: Charles and Sarah Wesley had eight children but only three—Charles, Jr., Sarah, and Samuel—survived infancy and childhood.)
1755		conference at which separation of Methodist societies from the Church of England is intensely debated; Charles strongly urges unity
1756		ends itinerant ministry and settles in Bristol; Conference reaffirms unity of the societies and the Church of England
1757	Dec. 11	son Charles is born
1759	Apr. 1	daughter Sarah is born
1762		publishes *Short Hymns on Select Passages of the Holy Scriptures*

1771		begins preaching regularly in London and moves to Chesterfield Street, Maryleborne, London
1778		City Road Chapel, London is opened
1788	Mar. 29	Charles Wesley dies
	Apr. 5	Charles Wesley is buried in Marylebone churchyard
1822	Dec. 22	Mrs. Charles Wesley dies

I

God

The power and blessing of God
can set all right.

Charles Wesley

1

Who Is God?

Come, O thou Traveller unknown,
  Whom still I hold, but cannot see!
My company before is gone,
  And I am left alone with thee,
With thee all night I mean to stay,
And wrestle till the break of day.

I need not tell thee who I am,
  My misery or sin declare;
Thyself hast called me by my name;
  Look on thy hands, and read it there:
But who, I ask thee, who art thou?
Tell me thy name, and tell me now.

In vain thou strugglest to get free;
  I never will unloose my hold!
Art thou the Man that died for me?
  The secret of thy love unfold;
Wrestling, I will not let thee go,
Till I thy name, thy nature know.

Wilt thou not yet to me reveal
  Thy new, unutterable name?
Tell me, I still beseech thee, tell;
  To know it now resolved I am;
Wrestling, I will not let thee go,
Till I thy name, thy nature know.

What though my shrinking flesh complain,
  And murmur to contend so long?
I rise superior to my pain,
  When I am weak, then I am strong;
And when my all of strength shall fail,
I shall with the God-Man prevail.

Yield to me now—for I am weak,
  But confident in self-despair;
Speak to my heart, in blessings speak,
  Be conquered by my instant prayer;

Speak, or thou never hence shalt move,
And tell me if thy name is Love.

'Tis Love! 'Tis Love! Thou diedst for me!
  I hear thy whisper in my heart.
The morning breaks, the shadows flee,
  Pure universal Love thou art;
To me, to all, thy mercies move,
Thy nature and thy name is Love.

My prayer has power with God; the grace
  Unspeakable I now receive;
Through faith I see thee face to face,
  I see thee face to face, and live!
In vain I have not wept, and strove:
Thy nature and thy name is Love.

I know thee, Savior, who thou art,
  Jesus, the feeble sinner's friend;
Nor wilt thou with the night depart,
  But stay, and love me to the end;
Thy mercies never shall remove:
Thy nature and thy name is Love.

The Sun of Righteousness on me
  Has risen with healing in his wings;
Withered my nature's strength, from Thee
  My soul is life and succour brings;
My help is all laid up above:
Thy nature and thy name is Love.

Contented now upon my thigh
  I halt, till life's short journey end;
All helplessness, all weakness, I
  On thee alone for strength depend;
Nor have I power from thee to move:
Thy nature and thy name is Love.

Lame as I am, I take the prey,
  Hell, earth, and sin with ease o'ercome;
I leap for joy, pursue my way,
  And as a bounding hart fly home,
Through all eternity to prove
Thy nature and thy name is Love.

—*Hymns and Sacred Poems* (1742)

With these lines Charles Wesley has written his autobiography. He sees the struggles of his own life mirrored in Jacob's wrestling with the angel. Wesley's life was a struggle to know the Unknown Traveller. Even after the revelation of May, 1738, when he grasped for the first time the reality of God's love for him in Jesus Christ, the struggle to know the heights and depths of such love and the God who gave and gives of self in that love continued until his death at age eighty-one.

This poem is not only his autobiography; it is ours as well. The questions he was asking are those we are asking:

Who is God?
  Who, I ask thee, who art thou? (stanza two)
Who is Jesus?
  Art thou the Man that died for me? (stanza three)
Can I know God?
  Wilt thou not yet to me reveal
  Thy new, unutterable name? (stanza four)

Wesley's search is our search, and it is the experience of faith which goes back for centuries.

We struggle to know the name and nature of God. We grasp for the Unknown, and we hold fast to that which we cannot see. Charles's brother John eloquently expressed the search for the unseen God in the translation of a German hymn by Gerhard Tersteegen:

Thou hidden love of God, whose height,
  Whose depth unfathomed, no one knows,
I see from far thy beauteous light,
  And inly sigh for thy repose;
My heart is pained, nor can it be
At rest, till it finds rest in thee.

The struggle is an identity crisis: Who is God and who am I? If I want divine vitality in my life, how can I receive it? In the Bible story, Jacob must first be asked who he is before he can receive the blessing. Wesley says, however:

I need not tell thee who I am,
My misery or sin declare;
Thyself hast called me by my name;
Look on thy hands, and read it there.

God knows the generations of humankind by name—"sinner"—and that name is written in the pierced hands of Jesus upon the cross. God knows who we are.

The struggle requires endurance.

Wrestling, I will not let thee go,
Till I thy name, thy nature know.

It is easy to give up in the midst of the struggle to know God. When we despair, lack confidence, and doubt, we must hold fast to the Unknown Traveller whom we cannot see, namely, God. We must "wrestle till the break of day," which is a lifelong struggle. This was Israel's experience. It is ours also. If we endure and do not let go, we will emerge from the struggle knowing that God's name and nature are one and the same: Love.

Stanzas one through six tell of the agony of the struggle, the mental and physical pain, and the soul-searching questions which often drive many away from God. Stanzas seven through twelve, however, describe the discovery of faith which resounds in the refrain: Thy nature and thy name is Love.

Love with a capital "L" is who God is, what God is like, and the way in which God's self-disclosure is revealed to us. It is God's love made known in Jesus which makes the shadows of doubt flee as dawn breaks and we confess with Wesley: "Pure, universal Love thou art!"

Who is God? Love. Who is Jesus? The One who shows us how God's love acts in the world. Can we know God? Yes! If we endure in the struggle to grasp God whom we cannot see, we will experience that love, God's love, acted out in life—which is what matters most.

2

What Is God's Will?

Thy will, O Lord, whate'er I do,
  My principle of action be.
Thy will I would through life pursue,
  Impelled, restrained, and ruled by thee;
And only think, and speak, and move,
As taught and guided by thy love.

—*Scripture Hymns* (1762)

How often we have heard that we are to do God's will, and yet we are not always certain we know what it is. Some would excise the freedom God has given human beings from the divine creative process and say that whatever happens is God's will. Hence, knowing God's will is simple. When you know what happens, you know God's will, because whatever happens is God's will. This, however, imposes evil, hatred, war, destruction, murder upon God's will in a way contrary to scripture and removes responsibility from human beings for their own actions and the evil which issues from human will.

Whatever happens is not God's will! To be sure, daily occurrences do not take place outside the context of God's will for love and wholeness for all people and the world at large. We can, however, oppose God's will and stand in its way.

This short poem stresses some important aspects of the role God's will is to play in our lives. First, it is to be the principle upon which we are to act. Second, it is to be the goal of our lives. God's will is something we seek all our lives long. It gives momentum to all we do. It restrains us and gives structure, form, and shape to our lives. And third, God's will guides our thoughts—even our words.

Those seem to be fine platitudes about God's will, but what is God's will? How can we *know* it in any given situation? What is God's will for my life vocationally? What is God's will for me when I am at school, at work, single, married, divorced, male, female, disabled, wronged, angry, poor, rich, unemployed? How do I know what the will of God is? Wesley suggests a way:

> And only think, and speak, and move,
> As taught and guided by thy love.

God's love should be the principle which shapes our understanding of God's will. How does that help us in knowing God's will? We know how God's love expressed itself. It was personified in Jesus, who willingly gave of himself in pursuit of others and their needs at all costs, even death upon a cross. In any situation in life we are to use the measure of God's love as expressed in Jesus as the means for determining our own actions.

What is God's will? It is the willingness to live out the principle of sacrificial love which goes in search of others at all costs, even to death. When we submit to that love, we will know God's will. When we love enough, we will know it.

3

Is God Dead?

O Love divine! What hast thou done!
  The immortal God hath died for me!
The Father's co-eternal Son
  Bore all my sins upon the tree;
The immortal God for me hath died!
My Lord, my Love is crucified.

Behold him, all ye that pass by,
  The bleeding Prince of life and peace!
Come, sinner, see your Maker die,
  And say, was ever grief like his?
Come, feel with me his blood applied:
My Lord, my Love is crucified.

Is crucified for me and you,
  To bring us rebels back to God;
Believe, believe the record true,
  Ye all are bought with Jesus' blood,
Pardon for all flows from his side:
My Lord, my Love is crucified.

Then let us sit beneath his cross,
  And gladly catch the healing stream,
All things for him account but loss,
  And give up all our hearts to him;
Of nothing think or speak beside,
"My Lord, my Love is crucified."

—*Hymns and Sacred Poems* (1749)

Some years ago there was much turmoil over the so-called death-of-God theology which hailed the inevitability of God's death. Although the popularity of this school of thought waned rather quickly, there was much discussion over the significance of a dying God and/or the death of the idea of God. It did bring Christians to a new realization that there is a death-of-God theology inherent in the scriptures. It has been eloquently summarized by Charles Wesley in the above hymn. Unfortunately, some hymn editors have changed the word "immortal" to "incarnate," but Wesley is expressing the mystery and wonder of the immortal Being who has created life and whose co-eternal Son dies on behalf of all humankind. In stanza two he phrases it another way: "Come, sinner, see your Maker die." The Creator dies for the created. (The editorial change of "Maker" to "Savior" in some hymnbooks radically changes Wesley's intention.)

The death of God has personal and universal implications, for the Son "bore all *my* sins upon the tree" but is "crucified for *me* and *you*." As particular and personal as his death may be for me, its effect is universal. It is a death for friends and enemies, peace lovers and war mongers, the loved and the hated, the moral and the immoral. God's death is not for saints but sinners. Hence, it is for all in order "to bring us rebels back to God."

When we see God's death in the context of creation, our own understanding of life and its complexities is more clearly focused. We view grief differently. All our pain and agony are seen against the backdrop of the excruciating death at Calvary and the groaning of the Creator for the whole of creation. "Was ever a grief like his?" Our complaints, sufferings, and sorrows are placed in proper perspective. Therefore, we will not break under them, for they are miniscule when seen in the light of our own Creator's suffering for us.

A woman arrived at her pastor's home one morning to begin her ritual of complaint about how people in the church and community were saying unkind and unjust things about her. When met at the door by the pastor's wife, she began her liturgy and hastily posed the question: "It simply is not right for anyone to be treated the way I am, is it?" The pastor's wife perceptively replied, "I don't know. They nailed Jesus to a cross." The woman was speechless. She paused, stutteringly offered a "good day," and departed. The death of God at Calvary places all our grief in proper perspective.

From beneath the cross we "catch the healing stream" and are made whole. We are cured of the illnesses of greed, malice, and lust as we grasp that "all things for him account but loss." Our hearts are no longer sick with false allegiances. The healing stream of God's love which flows from the cross restores them to health and singleness of purpose so that we think and speak only of one thing: "My Lord, my Love is crucified." A life of self-giving love, as we experience it in the crucifixion of Jesus, becomes the goal, purpose, and style of our lives.

4

What Is in a Name?

Thou hidden Source of calm repose
  Thou all-sufficient Love Divine,
My help and refuge from my foes,
  Secure I am, if thou art mine:
And lo, from sin and grief and shame,
I hide me, Jesus, in thy name.

Thy mighty name Salvation is,
  And keeps my happy soul above;
Comfort it brings and power and peace,
  And joy and everlasting love:
To me, with thy great name, are given
Pardon, and holiness, and heaven.

Jesus, my All in All thou art:
  My rest in toil, my ease in pain,
The med'cine of my broken heart,
  In war my peace, in loss my gain,
My smile beneath the tyrant's frown,
In shame my glory and my crown.

In want my plentiful supply,
  In weakness my almighty power,
In bonds my perfect liberty,
  My light in Satan's darkest hour,
In grief my joy unspeakable,
My life in death, my heaven in hell.

—*Hymns and Sacred Poems* (1749)

Charles Wesley claimed to have learned the love of knowledge from his mother and the virtue of sound study and the disciplines of hardship and denial from his father. From them both he learned the love of God. Even in moments of emptiness and despair it was this love which upheld him. Knowledge and experience taught him that God is the "all-sufficient Love Divine," who sustains us through all of life's haunting polarities and paradoxes.

Although the paradoxes of life often become stumbling blocks to faith, Wesley experienced God as the God of the paradoxes: God comes to us in the tensions and polarities of life with strength and wisdom that enable us to endure. When we feel there is no strength or reason to go on, we discover a hidden Source of power. Wesley tells us in stanza one that such power is all-sufficient Love Divine. It is our—

> help in weakness,
> refuge in desperation,
> security in insecurity,
> joy in grief;

and it imparts—

> sinlessness for sin,
> shamelessness for shame.

God is known by many names. One of the most powerful, we learn in stanza two, is Salvation, which is the meaning of Jesus' name, *Yeshu'a,* in Hebrew. We can experience the power of that name.

When someone who has been rescued from a disaster says to the rescuer, "You were my salvation!" that person knows the power and life-giving strength of being saved from death. Salvation imparts power, and the rescuer will always be known to the rescued as "salvation."

Wesley affirms that God is Salvation, having rescued us from destruction and given us a new life. God, our Salvation, brings—

> comfort when we are comfortless,
> power when we are powerless,
> peace when we suffer strife,
> joy when we are sad,
> love when we hate;

and imparts—

holiness for impurity,
heaven for hell.

Stanza three declares the discovery that Jesus is our All in All, for he personifies the all-sufficient Love Divine who seeks every human being at all costs. Those who follow this Jesus will find—

rest in toil,
ease in pain,
healing in broken hearts,
peace in war,
gain in loss,
smiles amid frowns,
glory amid shame.

Finally, in stanza four, we learn that faith in God's love as disclosed in Jesus brings—

abundance in want,
power in weakness,
liberty in bondage,
light in darkness,
life in death.

Wesley has eloquently summarized God's promises to all in this hymn, and his experience can be ours. We have only to trust the "hidden Source of calm repose" and follow the embodiment of all-sufficient divine love: Jesus.

5

How Do We Experience God?

The fire shall ever be burning upon the altar; it shall never go out.

—Leviticus 6:13, KJV

O thou who camest from above,
  The pure, celestial fire to impart,
Kindle a flame of sacred love
  On the mean altar of my heart;
There let it for thy glory burn
  With inextinguishable blaze,
And trembling to it's Source return,
  In humble prayer, and fervent praise.

Jesus, confirm my heart's desire
  To work, and speak, and think for thee,
Still let me guard the holy fire,
  And still stir up thy gift in me,
Ready for all thy perfect will
  My acts of faith and love repeat,
'Till death thy endless mercies seal,
  And make my sacrifice complete.

—*Scripture Hymns* (1762)

It is reported that in John Wesley's later years some preachers came to him to inquire about his experience of God, reminding him that often he had asked them to share their own experiences. His reply is said to have been the quotation of the last stanza of "O thou who camest from above." What an insightful summary that stanza is of the Christian's experience of God.

We experience God by working, speaking, and thinking for God. As Christians we pray daily:

Jesus, confirm my heart's desire
  To work, and speak, and think for thee,
Still let me guard the holy fire,
  And still stir up thy gift in me.

The holy fire which Wesley would guard is the "flame of sacred love" of which he speaks in stanza one. Love is the source of activity, speech, and thought. What a transforming power it is when all we do, say, and think issues from love! The world has yet to experience such total transformation of all people. Yet, those who have the courage and vision to follow Jesus know and experience its possibility and reality.

We also experience God by constantly being alert to God's will. This we do by repeating acts of faith and love all our lives. Our best experience of God's will and the way we know it most certainly is by acting out faith and love. It is a lifelong activity:

> Till death thy endless mercies seal
> And make my sacrifice complete.

Both John and Charles Wesley understood life as a sacrifice. Like Paul, they experienced dying daily with Christ. Calvary's cross became for them and becomes for us a pattern of life: give all we have, all our lives, in love for God and others. That is what Jesus did. His sacrifice shapes our own. This motivated John to form some simple rules for living:

> Do all the good you can,
> By all the means you can,
> In all the ways you can,
> In all the places you can,
> At all the times you can,
> To all the people you can
> As long as ever you can.

If we act out faith and love as followers of Jesus, we will know God's will.

II

Jesus

One look of Jesus Christ
can break your heart this moment,
and bind it up by faith.

Charles Wesley

6

Who Is Jesus?

Savior of all, what hast thou done?
  What hast thou suffered on the tree?
Why didst thou groan thy mortal groan,
  Obedient unto death for me?
The myst'ry of thy passion show,—
The end of all thy griefs below.

Pardon, and grace, and heaven to buy,
  My bleeding sacrifice expired:
But didst thou not my pattern die,
  That, by thy glorious Spirit fired,
Faithful to death I might endure,
And make the crown by suffering sure?

Thou didst the meek example leave,
  That I might in thy footsteps tread;
Might like the Man of Sorrows grieve,
  And groan, and bow with thee my Head:
Thy dying in my body bear,
And all thy state of suff'ring share.

—*Hymns and Sacred Poems* (1749)

Sometimes we are asked, "Who has been the greatest influence in your life?" Usually we respond with the name of someone we know or have known during our lifetime: father, mother, teacher, coach, friend. It is often someone who has inspired and encouraged us, fostered our talents and abilities, given us a set of values by which to live, or been a model of character and purpose after which to pattern our lives. How often do we answer that Christ is the most influential person in our lives?

Wesley asks, "But didst thou not *my pattern* die?" It is common to think of Christ as an example of goodness and virtue, as someone who went about doing good. Wesley suggests, however, that Christ's pattern for our lives has a much deeper meaning than that. The overarching pattern he gives us for living is one of suffering and dying. It is the cruciform life in that it draws its form, meaning, and energy from the crucifixion. This is the key to the example of life Christ sets before us.

The apostle Paul understood the cruciform life when he said, "I die daily" (1 Corinthians 15:31). Wesley comprehended it when he wrote, "Thy dying in my body bear." Christians bear the death of Christ in themselves. Like Christ, they are to be faithful through suffering even unto and until death. That is at the heart of Christ's pattern of life. Suffering does not bring faith into question; it affirms it! Christ demonstrates its importance in redeeming and reclaiming life. Suffering crowns existence: "And make the crown by suffering sure."

The shallow quest for "happiness" often involves the attempt to avoid suffering, but suffering is an integral part of living. That is a mystery, just as the redemptive power of Christ's passion, death, and resurrection is a mystery. Yet, suffering is a reality. And when we open ourselves to the mystery of Christ's redemption, the anguish of earthly life is relieved. We are able to endure faithfully to the end.

To pattern our lives after Calvary does not mean we are to have martyr complexes. Rather, it means that suffering and death do not defeat us. They renew, redeem, and reclaim us as do the suffering and death of Christ.

7

Why Was Jesus Born?

Lo, he comes with clouds descending,
  Once for favored sinners slain;
Thousand, thousand saints attending,
  Swell the triumph of his train:
    Hallelujah,
  God appears on earth to reign!

Every eye shall now behold him
  Robed in dreadful majesty;
Those who set at nought and sold him,
  Pierced and nailed him to the tree,
    Deeply wailing,
  Shall the true Messiah see.

The dear tokens of his passion
  Still his dazzling body bears;
Cause of endless exultation
  To his ransomed worshippers;
    With what rapture
  Gaze we on those glorious scars.

Yea, amen! let all adore thee
  High on thine eternal throne;
Savior, take the power and glory
  Claim the kingdom for thine own:
    Hallelujah,
  Everlasting God, come down.

—*Hymns of Intercession for all Mankind* (1758)

This hymn, which anticipates Christ's coming in glory, is often appropriately sung during the Advent season, but it expresses the Christian's hope at every time of the year. Every day is filled with the expectation of Christ's advent. Wesley tells us why.

Sinners are transformed into saints (stanza one).

Thousand, thousand saints attending,
Swell the triumph of his train.

To the One who was slain for sinners they cry out: "Hallelujah!" This is quite a different picture from the small band of adoring shepherds at Bethlehem and the wise men who followed. Even if the angels resounded, "Glory to God in the highest," thousands of saints did not hail Christ's birth. As Christians continue to pray with the early church, "Come, Lord Jesus," they do so with the confidence that God transforms a small band of worshipers at Bethlehem into thousands upon thousands worldwide resounding, "Hallelujah!" at Christ's coming in glory. History and people are changed! Sinners have now become saints through the redemptive life, ministry, death, and resurrection of Jesus Christ.

Narrow human vision is transformed into God's universal vision (stanza two). Human exclusivity becomes God's inclusivity. All "shall the true Messiah see." It is not a select few who will have this vision. "Every eye shall now behold him;" even Judas who sold him for thirty pieces of silver and the soldiers who pierced his side with a spear and drove the nails through his hands and feet at Calvary shall see Christ for who he truly is: the Messiah. God's most illuminating view of life will be seen by those with the poorest vision.

Suffering is transformed into exultation (stanza three). Calvary, the symbol of pain, agony, and death gives cause for jubilation to all who worship Christ, for they have experienced redemption and release from their sins. As they "gaze...on those glorious scars," which become symbolic of life, not death, they begin to experience that God transforms life's suffering into joy.

The world's weakness is transformed into God's strength (stanza four). Throughout history, nations, leaders, and peoples have sought to claim the kingdoms of the earth as their own. The results have been appalling: greed, war, destruction, wealth and poverty, the powerful and the powerless, masters and servants, and on it goes. The Christian's hope is that in the coming of Christ, God lays claim to the kingdom of the earth establishing love as the reigning power throughout the world. That day has not yet arrived, and we continue to pray, "Come, Lord Jesus!"

Everlasting God, come down.

Come and transform—

sinners into saints,
narrow vision into universal vision,
suffering into joy,
weakness into strength.

8

Can We Believe the Mystery?

When he did our flesh assume
  That everlasting Man,
Mary held him in her womb
  Whom heaven could not contain!
Who the mystery can believe!
  Incomprehensible thou art;
Yet we still by faith conceive,
  And bear thee in our heart.

—*Scripture Hymns* (1762)

"The Word became flesh and dwelt among us" (John 1:14, RSV). Who can explain God's assumption of human flesh in the form of Jesus? Who can explain Mary's conception of the Holy Child? These mysteries are unfathomable to the human mind.

Who the mystery can believe!
  Incomprehensible thou art.

We cannot subject the mystery to scientific analysis for verification. There are realities which transcend logic and science. We may say that we love someone and vow that such love is real, but we cannot prove it. Love transcends proof. We may produce what we view as tangible evidence of love, but the evidence is not the love itself. Love's reality resides within us. We can communicate that reality in our thoughts, words, actions, and emotions—in who we are. We personify love's reality.

The scripture tells us that "God is love" (1 John 4:8). In other words, God is best defined or described as Love, and Jesus personifies the reality of Love, Supreme Love, which goes in search of all human beings at all costs, even to death upon a cross. Jesus is the evidence that Love is real. Through the indwelling

Spirit of Jesus, Love's reality resides within us. And though we do not fully comprehend it,

> Yet we still by faith conceive
> And bear thee in our heart.

9

Can We Live the Mystery?

And can it be that I should gain
  An interest in the Savior's blood?
Died he for me, who caused his pain?
  For me, who him to death pursued?
Amazing love! How can it be
That thou, my God, shouldst die for me?

'Tis mystery all: the Immortal dies!
  Who can explore the strange design?
In vain the first-born seraph tries
  To sound the depths of love divine.
'Tis mercy all! Let earth adore,
Let angel minds enquire no more.

He left his Father's throne above—
  So free, so infinite his grace—
Emptied himself of all but love,
  And bled for Adam's helpless race.
'Tis mercy all, immense and free;
For, O my God, it found out me!

Long my imprisoned spirit lay
  Fast bound in sin and nature's night;
Thine eye diffused a quickening ray—
  I woke, the dungeon flamed with light,
My chains fell off, my heart was free,
I rose, went forth, and followed thee.

No condemnation now I dread;
  Jesus, and all in him, is mine!
Alive in him, my living Head,
  And clothed in righteousness divine,
Bold I approach the eternal throne,
And claim the crown, through Christ,
  my own.

—*Hymns and Sacred Poems* (1739)

The soul-searching questions of stanza one above

characterize Wesley's lifelong quest for God from his earliest search to his constant realization that this "interest" was indeed the consuming passion of his life. They reflect his spiritual journey and personalize Christian experience. Therefore, if we consider these questions carefully, our relationship to God will grow and Wesley's questions will become ours.

> And can it be that I should gain
> An interest in the Savior's blood?

Wesley was astounded that he should be interested in Christ's sacrifice. The events of Calvary had occurred centuries ago. What should draw his attention to them now? He had reluctantly become an Anglican clergyman in 1735 at the insistence of his brother John, whom he then accompanied with great reservation to the American colony of Georgia as a member of Oglethorpe's staff and as a missionary. He had thought of spending all his days at Oxford. It was there he had taken his degrees and established himself as a lecturer of Christ Church. Life at Oxford had won his interest. Yet, something was lacking. On board the ship *Simmonds* just off the Island of Tibey in Georgia he wrote:

> In vain have I fled from myself to America. I still groan under the intolerable weight of inherent misery! If I have never yet repented of my undertaking, it is because I could hope for nothing better in England—or Paradise. Go where I will I carry my own Hell about me.[1]

In 1736 Charles Wesley returned to England despondent over his ineffectiveness in Georgia. There was tremendous inner turmoil in his life. It was not until May 21, 1738, that the answer "Yes!" came to the question:

> Died he for me, who caused his pain?
> For me, who him to death pursued?

As he read Martin Luther's commentary on Galatians, especially the conclusion to chapter two, Wesley knew that his own sin was a part of the sin of all humankind for which Christ had given his life on the cross. Therefore, he confessed, "Amazing love!" Wesley had experienced the social evils of his day in England with its outcast, destitute, hungering masses and those of America with its dastardly enslavement of blacks. Now he realized that the sacrifice of Christ at Calvary had been made for those sins; but not for social sins only, for they have their origin in personal sin.

Wesley would spend the rest of his life in wonder over God's amazing love, knowing that he could never fully comprehend it. It would be a constant struggle. Over a year after his conversion he wrote in his *Journal:*

> I never knew till now the strength of temptation, and energy of sin. Who, that conferred with flesh and blood, would covet great success? I live in continual storm. My soul is always in my hand. The enemy thrusts sore at me, that I may fall; and a worse enemy than the devil is my own heart.... I received, I humbly hope, a fresh pardon in the sacrament at St. Paul's.
>
> —*Journal,* vol. I, p. 157

'Tis mystery all: the Immortal dies!
Who can explore his strange design?

Wesley learned to live the mystery: that questions and confession go together; that to be emptied of everything but love is what it means to serve a God who in Christ "emptied himself of all but love."

If Charles Wesley's questions are our questions, let his realizations and his confession be ours as well. Let us learn to live the mystery of God's love. In moments when we feel the emptiest, let us boldly "approach the eternal throne" knowing:

'Tis mercy all, immense and free,
For, O my God, it found out me.

---

1. Frank Baker, *Charles Wesley As Revealed by His Letters* (London: Epworth, 1948) p. 22.

10

Was Jesus Born to Set *All* People Free?

Come, thou long-expected Jesus,
  Born to set thy people free;
From our fears and sins release us;
  Let us find our rest in thee.
Israel's strength and consolation,
  Hope of all the earth thou art;
Dear desire of every nation,
  Joy of every longing heart.

Born thy people to deliver,
  Born a child and yet a King,
Born to reign in us forever,
  Now thy gracious kingdom bring.
By thine own eternal spirit
  Rule in all our hearts alone;
By thine all-sufficient merit,
  Raise us to thy glorious throne.

—*Nativity Hymns* (1745)

This great hymn of freedom and deliverance takes on added dimensions of meaning when we consider one particular occurrence in Charles Wesley's life. Spent and dejected after only five months in the colony of Georgia, he decided to return to England. Charles made his way overland to Charleston where the boat he was to board for England would set sail. But if his spirits were at a low ebb, they were utterly shattered by his firsthand encounter with slavery upon arrival in Charleston. He recorded it in his *Journal*.

> I had observed much, and heard more, of the cruelty of masters towards their negroes, but I received an authentic account of some horrid instances thereof at Charleston before I set out on my return voyage to England. . . . The giving a child a slave of its own to tyrannize, to beat and abuse out of sport, was, I myself saw, a common practice. Nor is it strange, being thus trained up in cruelty,

> they should afterwards arrive at so great perfection in it; that Mr. Star, a gentleman I often met at Mr. Lasserre's, should, as he himself informed Lasserre, first nail up a negro by the ears, then order him to be whipped in the severest manner, and then to have scalding water thrown over him, so that the poor creature could not stir for four months after....
>
> These horrid cruelties are the less to be wondered at, because the government itself, in effect, countenances and allows them to kill their slaves, by the ridiculous penalty appointed for it, of about seven pounds sterling, half of which is usually saved by the criminal's informing against himself. This I can look upon as no other than a public act to indemnify murder.
>
> —*Journal* vol. I, pp. 36–37

As this hymn declares, Charles Wesley knew that Jesus was born to set all people free; yes, the slaves too! Mortified by the terror of slavery, he could only hope that slaves, their masters, and all touched by this savage villainy could be set free from fears and sins and find their rest in Jesus. "This is the only hope of all the earth," Wesley cries out. He understood and had experienced that Jesus was truly born to deliver people from bondage and that when he ruled their hearts, they could no longer subject others to the tyranny of servitude.

In a world teeming with injustice we need to sing this hymn with great expectancy and live its message until those who are enslaved to sin and all human bondage are set free!

Come, thou long-expected Jesus!

III

Faith

Faith is the life of the soul.

Charles Wesley

11

Can We Prove Faith?

Ye different sects who all declare,
"Lo! Here is Christ!" or "Christ is there!"
Your stronger proofs divinely give,
And show me where the Christians live!

—*Hymns and Sacred Poems* (1749)

The Flemish Quietist, Antoinette Bourignon, tells a childhood story in her autobiography in which she relates her dissatisfaction with life around her after reading the gospels. She realized that the environment in which she lived was not modeled after Jesus' example of love and selflessness. Therefore, she asked her parents, "Where are the Christians? Let us go to the country where the Christians live." Wesley is thought to have recalled her words when he wrote these powerful lines.

There is no age of Christianity which has not been riddled with dissension. Throughout history, councils of the church have sought to make doctrinal decisions on what authenticates the Christian faith and the Christian church. One need only list the primary emphases of major branches or churches in Christendom to grasp what have been seen traditionally as its "stronger proofs." Nevertheless, often overemphasis of such "proofs" has led to the division of the church. One need only think of common misconceptions Christians sometimes have of one another. "Roman Catholics *believe* in relics." "Presbyterians *believe* in predestination." "Methodists *believe* in falling from grace." "Baptists *believe* in the evil of dancing and movies." Unquestionably, all such misconceptions have their origin in an over-emphasis of some aspect of faith's expression.

Wesley tells us that we cannot prove the faith by what we affirm, but we can demonstrate its effectiveness by how we live. Our task is not to show others what Christians believe but where Christians live!

12

How Do We Relate What We Believe to What We Do?

Not slothful in business, fervent in spirit, serving the Lord.

—Romans 12:11, KJV

Their earthly task who fail to do
Neglect their heavenly business too,
Nor know what faith and duty mean,
Who use religion as a screen,
Asunder put what God hath joined,
A diligent and pious mind.

Full well the labor of our hands
With fervency of spirit stands;
For God, who all our days hath given,
From toil excepts but one in seven;
And laboring, while we time redeem,
We let the work our God esteem.

Happy we live, when God doth fill
Our hands with work, our hearts with zeal;
For every toil, if God enjoin,
Becomes a sacrifice divine,
And like the blessed spirits above
The more we serve, the more we love.

—*Scripture Hymns* (1762)

An uncle of mine once preached a sermon on faith and works entitled, "With Which Wing Does a Bird Fly?" Obviously the answer was, "With neither one or the other but with both." Likewise for the Christian, faith and works are not self-exclusive. Both are necessary to a balanced walk in Christ. Saying that we understand the meaning of faith without doing faith's duty means we make out of our religion a screen. The side others see may look beautiful and impressive, but behind it there is emptiness, disarray, and confusion.

God does not intend that we make such breaches in our behavior, characters, and personalities. God does not intend that we separate diligence and piety but that we mold them into an enduring unity.

Upon the death of Heinrich Boell, the German writer who received a Nobel Peace Prize for literature in 1972, one of his friends, a clergyman, said of him, "He was one of the very few persons I have ever known for whom belief and action were totally synonymous." Boell, who became extremely active after World War II in opposing oppression of people in any form and was engaged in the peace movement, knew that the only test of belief is the arena of action.

We experience the viability and validity of faith only by acting on it, by doing the radical things faith demands—such as loving our enemies, doing good to those who use us spitefully, loving our neighbors as we love ourselves, going out in complete trust not knowing where we are going, aiding the poor, feeding the hungry, caring for the sick and dying. Faith offers no alternatives to fulfilling these demands. Indeed they are faith's duty.

The apostle Paul gave the church at Rome a threefold formula for maintaining the balance of faith and works: (1) take responsible action in all you do, (2) be fervent in spirit, and (3) serve God. Utilizing a vocabulary of active verbs will do much for discovering faith's response. Faith may involve understanding, but faith is by no means a static noun or state. Faith is action. People of faith serve and love God and others. How true that "the more we serve, the more we love."

If we do not do faith's duty, we make of our religion a screen hiding our emptiness, disarray, and confusion.

13

What Is Eternal Life?

"Christ the Lord is risen today,"
Sons of men and angels say;[1]
Raise your joys and triumphs high;
Sing, ye heavens, and earth reply.

Love's redeeming work is done;
Fought the fight, the battle won;
Lo! our Sun's eclipse is o'er,
Lo! He sets in blood no more.

Vain the stone, the watch, the seal;
Christ has burst the gates of hell!
Death in vain forbids his rise:
Christ has opened Paradise!

Lives again our glorious King;
Where, O death, is now thy sting?
Dying once, he all doth save;[2]
Where thy victory, O grave?

Soar we now where Christ has led,
Following our exalted Head;
Made like him, like him we rise,
Ours the cross, the grave, the skies!

Hail the Lord of earth and heaven!
Praise to thee by both be given;
Thee we greet triumphant now;
Hail the Resurrection thou!

King of glory, soul of bliss,
Everlasting life is this:
Thee to know, thy power to prove,
Thus to sing, and thus to love!

—*Hymns and Sacred Poems* (1739)

This popular and powerful hymn on the resurrection of Christ was originally entitled by Wesley, "Hymn for Easter Day." When first published in 1739, it included eleven stanzas. The seven above are those which appear most frequently in hymnbooks, although often they have been edited and rearranged.

When we sing or read this hymn, we catch the spirit of the resurrection and go on a journey through a vast spectrum of emotions and thoughts which issue from and surround Christ's resurrection. All creation joins in the refrain:

"Christ the Lord is risen today."

All creation sings, for love has defeated death! The darkness which shrouded the crucifixion has vanished, and no more must blood be shed to redeem humankind (see stanzas one and two).

No human effort can contain God's mighty act to open Paradise to all creation (stanza three). Hence, Paul's questions in First Corinthians, "O death, where is thy sting? O grave, where is thy victory?" (15:55, KJV) are preceded by the following affirmations:

Lives again our glorious King;
. . . .
Dying once, he all doth save.

We too rise with Christ: "Soar we now where Christ has led." He has gone before us and shown us our destiny which is summarized in three words: "Ours the *cross,* the *grave,* the *skies.*" We suffer, die, and rise with Christ.

Unquestionably the church was born out of the resurrection faith and hope of life eternal. To be sure, this hymn eloquently proclaims that faith and hope. Wesley did not intend, however, to end the hymn merely on the note of hope in the resurrection faith and everlasting life, as many hymnbooks do by excluding the concluding two stanzas of the original hymn. They are stanzas six and seven here. The hymn ends as it has begun—in praise of the risen Christ. Yet there is more. It affirms that everlasting life is a present possession, not merely a future reward. Furthermore, it takes on a tangible form—now.

King of glory, soul of bliss,
Everlasting life is this:
Thee to *know,* thy power to *prove,*
Thus to *sing,* and thus to *love.*

Wesley uses verbs to describe everlasting life because it is active life in the present. What is eternal life?

Thee to know. Wesley remembers Jesus' prayer in John 17:3: "This is eternal life, that they know thee the only true God, and Jesus Christ whom thou hast sent" (RSV). Eternal life involves an active mental process. First John 5:20 expresses it this way: "We know that the Son of God has come and has given us understanding, to know him who is true; and we are in him who is true, in his Son Jesus Christ. This is the true God and eternal life" (RSV).

Thy power to prove. Eternal life is proving God's power. Wesley does not mean we are to verify God's power; rather, we are to personify such power and be its proof, its testimony in a world which prefers to trust its own power.

Thus to sing. Eternal life is singing creation's hymn of praise to the Creator who has obliterated the force of death which would threaten creation. As Augustine once said, "The Christian must be an Alleluia from head to foot." That is the eternal song!

Thus to love. Eternal life is loving as Christ loved, even if it means sacrificing one's life. It is a perpetually self-giving love, which goes in search of others and God at all costs, even death.

Christians are active participants in everlasting life now. "Christ the Lord is risen today" and so are we! This is our hymn for Easter and every day of the year.

---

1. Erik Routley suggests the effective inclusive phrase "all creation joins to say" for this line. See *Rejoice in the Lord,* edited by Erik Routley (Grand Rapids: W. B. Eerdmans, 1985) Nr. 325.

2. The manuscript Richmond Tracts shows this line in Charles Wesley's handwriting in the following (and probably later) version: "Once He died our Souls to save." It appears in many subsequent hymnbooks.

14

What Do We Really Want?

Jesus, lover of my soul,
  Let me to thy bosom fly,
While the nearer waters roll,
  While the tempest still is high.
Hide me, O my Savior, hide,
  Till the storm of life is past:
Safe into the haven guide;
  O receive my soul at last.

Other refuge have I none:
  Hangs my helpless soul on thee.
Leave, ah leave me not alone,
  Still support and comfort me.
All my trust on thee is stayed,
  All my help from thee I bring;
Cover my defenceless head
  With the shadow of thy wing.

Wilt thou not regard my call?
  Wilt thou not accept my prayer?
Lo, on thee I cast my care.
  Lo, I sink, I faint, I fall!
Reach me out thy gracious hand!
  While I of thy strength receive,
Hoping against hope I stand,
  Dying, and behold I live!

Thou, O Christ, art all I want;
  More than all in thee I find.
Raise the fallen, cheer the faint,
  Heal the sick, and lead the blind.
Just and holy is thy Name;
  I am all unrighteousness:
False and full of sin I am;
  Thou art full of truth and grace.

Plenteous grace with thee is found,
  Grace to cover all my sin:
Let the healing streams abound,

Make and keep me pure within.
Thou of life the fountain art;
Freely let me take of thee:
Spring thou up within my heart,
Rise to all eternity.

—*Hymns and Sacred Poems* (1740)

The distinguished preacher Henry Ward Beecher once said, "I would rather have written 'Jesus, lover of my soul' than to have the fame of all the kings that ever lived."

Like many of Charles Wesley's poems, "Jesus, lover of my soul" takes on new meaning when understood against the backdrop of his own experience and the time in which he lived. While we do not know the specific date of its composition, we know it was published in 1740 at a time of great conflict in England and within the Church of England. The imagery of this poem grows out of the crises of the period. The Wesley brothers were often beaten, stoned, and run out of town. By virtue of their affiliation with the university, they assumed an itinerant ministry and traveled from town to town, village to village, and parish to parish, which roused the ire of many clergy and laity. In the face of violent opposition, Charles indeed hoped for a time when "the storm of life is past." Often in the midst of a riotous mob he knew that "other refuge have I none" and that he bore a "defenceless head" except God should cover it.

The third stanza does not appear in most hymnbooks. But it is most important, for it alone places before us Wesley's agonizing questions, so often a part of his most significant lyrics.

Wilt thou not regard my call?
Wilt thou not accept my prayer?

Wesley understood the anguish of rejection. Often he was called a Papist, a Jesuit, a Dissenter and on one occasion was falsely accused of treason, a charge dismissed by a judge before whom Wesley eloquently defended himself. The agony of his thoughts as to whether God would reject him in the same manner human beings had done was overcome only by the confidence in his plea:

> Reach me out thy gracious hand!
>   While I of thy strength receive,
> Hoping against hope I stand,
>   Dying, and behold I live.

The sustenance of God's grace was Wesley's fountain of strength. In this poem he helps us to see that nothing but total commitment to Christ enables us to drink from that fountain. Here is how.

> All my trust on thee is stayed,
>   All my help from thee I bring.

We may place our trust in others, our families, nations, governments, lifestyles, laws, wealth, professions, vocations. It is God alone, however, who will sustain us in adversity, temptation, danger, and death.

> Lo, on thee I cast my care.

We prefer to cast our cares on others because we are weak, irresponsible, apathetic, or spiteful. Only when we cast our cares on God do we find one who makes the burden bearable.

> Thou, O Christ, art all I want.

To know what we *want* is of primary importance every day we live. Perhaps the origin of much unhappiness, much paranoia, and many neuroses is that people have no idea what they want. Wesley focused on a singular *want*—Christ. There is the key. The question becomes not "*What* do we want?" but "*Whom* do we want?" Once we want only Christ, we begin to find out what we want to do in and with our lives.

15

Where Do We Start?

Where shall my wondering soul begin?
  How shall I all to heaven aspire?
A slave redeemed from death and sin,
  A brand plucked from eternal fire,
How shall I equal triumphs raise,
Or sing my great deliverer's praise?

O how shall I the goodness tell,
  Father, which thou to me hast showed?
That I, a child of wrath and hell,
  I should be called a child of God,
Should know, should feel my sins forgiven,
Blest with this antepast of heaven!

And shall I slight my Father's love?
  Or basely fear his gifts to own?
Unmindful of his favors prove?
  Shall I, the hallowed cross to shun,
Refuse his righteousness to impart
By hiding it within my heart?

Outcasts of men, to you I call,
  Harlots, and publicans, and thieves!
He spreads his arms to embrace you all;
  Sinners alone his grace receives:
No need of him the righteous have;
He came the lost to seek and save.

Come all ye Magdalens in lust,
  Ye ruffians fell in murders old;
Repent, and live: despair and trust!
  Jesus for you to death was sold.
Though hell protest, and earth repine,
He died for crimes like yours—and mine.

Come, O my guilty sinners, come,
  Groaning beneath your load of sin!
His bleeding heart shall make you room,
  His open side shall take you in;
He calls you now, invites you home:
Come, O my guilty sinners, come!

—*Hymns and Sacred Poems* (1739)

Charles Wesley called this poem his conversion hymn. He wrote it just two days after a life-transforming encounter with Christ which he described in his journal. "I now found myself at peace with God, and rejoiced in hope of loving Christ.... I saw that by faith I stood" (May 21, 1738). He continued, "At nine [on May 23] I began an hymn upon my conversion, but was persuaded to break off, for fear of pride. Mr. Bray coming, encouraged me to proceed in spite of Satan. I prayed Christ to stand by me and finished the hymn."

The following evening his brother John went to a meeting at Aldersgate Street in London where, during the reading of Martin Luther's Preface to the Epistle to the Romans, he felt his heart strangely warmed and that he trusted Christ alone for salvation. After the meeting Charles records, "Towards ten, my brother was brought in triumph by a troop of our friends, and declared, 'I believe.' We sang the hymn ['Where Shall My Wondering Soul Begin?'] with great joy, and parted with prayer."

Often so-called conversion hymns reflect a self-centered kind of assurance which Charles Wesley would have found displeasing. He helps us understand how to respond to such an experience.

First, be overcome with awe and wonder. Where do we begin once we have made a commitment to Christ? How can we aspire to heaven or even have the audacity to praise God when we know we are unworthy and weak? There is the beginning place—to admit our own sinfulness.

Second, want to tell the story of redemption, but do so only after much soul-searching—and never cheaply. Ask, How shall we tell of God's goodness? If we do not share this story, do we not slight God's love, prove ourselves unmindful of God's favor, and avoid the cross of Christ? Tell the story.

Third, begin with the most unlikely people: prostitutes, thieves, murderers. Christ "died for crimes like yours—and mine." So often the church has not begun its work among the most unlikely. It can learn from Christ, from its past, and from Wesley. Think of those persons who would be the most unlikely to hear anyone tell and live out the story of redemption and begin with them.

And finally, personify repentance, trust, and belief. We make our lives arguments for Christ by being repentant, by trusting, and by showing our belief in God, in what we think, say, and do. Then others will hunger for the love and forgiveness of God they see in us.

16

How Do We Read the Bible?

Come, Holy Ghost, our hearts inspire,
  Let us thy influence prove;
Source of the old prophetic fire,
  Fountain of life, and love.

Come, Holy Ghost, (for, moved by thee
  Thy prophets wrote and spoke:)
Unlock thy truth, thyself the key,
  Unseal the sacred book.

Expand thy wings, prolific dove,
  Brood o'er our nature's night;
On our disordered Spirits move,
  And let there now be light.

Through God's own self we then shall know
  If thou within us shine,
And sound, with all thy saints below,
  The depths of love divine.

—*Hymns and Sacred Poems* (1740)

There may be many simple messages in the Bible, but the Bible is by no means a simple book. It spans numerous centuries and is not written in chronological order. To grasp its message and meaning, some knowledge of the world from which it came, the ancient Near East, is essential. It is written in three languages—Hebrew, Aramaic, and Greek—and all who do not read them must read translations. As faithful as translators try to be to the original languages in the form they have received them in the biblical books, it is not always easy to capture the nuances of idioms, expressions, and words for which there are no direct equivalents in many languages.

Serious students of the Bible use every possible means to study it. For example, the young science of archeology has yielded a wealth of information which greatly enhances the understanding of the world, language, history, and message of the Bible. Unquestionably diverse avenues of investigation and research have developed in biblical studies which illuminate the Bible. Nevertheless, the scripture embodies a quality which transcends and complements all methods of its study. While many of them prove useful in appropriating the Bible in order to glean the most authentic meaning possible, the scripture has a self-appropriating power: an ability to find people where they are and to speak to them and their needs.

Wesley's hymn, "Come, Holy Ghost, our hearts inspire," affirms an approach to the Bible which allows its self-appropriating quality to empower and enlarge our understanding of God's word. Regardless of the method or tools utilized to study the Bible, there must be an inner openness to allow God's Spirit to speak through the word. There is a divine influence which pours from its pages into our lives: "Let us thy influence prove." Wesley bids us prayerfully seek that influence as we read the Bible, for it is the source of God's past and present inspiration and the "fountain of life, and love."

The "influence" is God's own Spirit which moves throughout the scripture with a dynamism that imparts truth.

> Unlock thy truth, thyself the key
> Unseal the sacred book.

Those who find their lives shattered and desperate can search the scriptures and discover the truth about God, themselves, and their needs which heals and makes new beginnings possible.

God's Spirit not only unlocks the truth of scripture, it sheds light upon the darkness of our lives. It brings order to disordered spirits.

> On our disordered spirits move,
> And let there now be light.

Stanza four affirms that it is God's own self that is revealed through the scriptures, and thus it is God whom we come to know as we read them. The light which floods our lives from the pages of the Bible is God's own radiance.

How do we read the Bible? In an attitude of prayer with heart and being open to the Spirit's influence, truth, and light. In so doing we sound the depths of love divine. Ships make soundings to determine the depth of the water. When we read the Bible, we are sounding the depths of divine love. Its depths cannot be determined, however, as one measures the depth of water to the ocean floor, for God's love is fathomless. Nevertheless, each time we read the Bible with openness to God's Spirit, we shall discover new depths of that love. The deeper we go into God's word, the deeper we plunge into God's love. In Jesus, divine love ascends a cross, goes down to a grave, and rises to earth and heaven for us.

Each time we read the Bible we search for God's love. Hence, the act itself becomes an act of love!

IV

Others and the World

It is then the best time
to labor for our neighbor,
when we are most cast down,
and most unable to keep ourselves.

Charles Wesley

17

Do We Care about Others?

I have showed you all things, how that so laboring ye ought to support the weak, and to remember the words of the Lord Jesus, how he said, "It is more blessed to give than to receive."

—Acts 20:35, KJV

Your duty let the Apostle show
Ye ought, ye ought to labor so,
In Jesus cause employed,
Your calling's works at times pursue,
And keep the tent-maker in view,
And use your hands for God.

Work for the weak, and sick and poor,
Raiment and food for them procure,
And mindful of God's Word,
Enjoy the blessedness to give,
Lay out your gettings, to relieve
The members of your Lord.

Your labor which proceeds from love,
Jesus shall graciously approve,
With full felicity
With brightest crowns your loan repay,
And tell you in that joyful day,
"Ye did it unto me."

—*Manuscript Acts*

As Paul bids farewell to the elders of Ephesus, he makes clear to them that his work among them was not for personal gain: "I coveted no one's silver or gold or apparel. You yourselves know that these hands ministered to my necessities, and to those who were with me" (Acts 20:33–34, RSV). Then he reminds them that they should support the weak in their labors, remembering Jesus' words, "It is more blessed to give than to receive."

Using our hands for God is part of the Christian's

calling. How often we seek other ways to work for God than manual labor! It is often easier to give our money, lip-service, or even lend our names to support some cause. Wesley says to keep Paul in mind as your example of a servant of Jesus, "and use your hands for God." It is one thing to give a sizable check to buy food for a soup kitchen for the needy. It is quite another to go and pour the soup into the bowls. Both are necessary, and neither excludes the other.

Service to others was the foundation of Wesley's lifestyle from his days at Oxford, when he began taking food for body and spirit to prisoners, a practice he continued throughout his life. Whether it was founding an orphanage or beginning a school for the children of poor miners, Wesley sought to follow the example of Christ and the apostle Paul in laboring for the less fortunate. His brother John even founded a medical dispensary for those who could not afford proper medical care.

It is a mandate of the gospel: "Support the weak!" It is not an option for the Christian; it is a duty. When we are mindful of Jesus' words about giving, we will enjoy the blessedness which accompanies it.

In verse three Wesley points out the origin and focus of our labor—it "proceeds from love." It is love which necessitates, motivates, and precipitates our work for ourselves and others. When we give of our labor to the weak, sick, and poor, we give it to Christ. When we withhold it, we withhold it from Christ. "If you are ashamed of poverty, you are ashamed of your Master,"[1] says Wesley.

If we begin each day with the same feeling once expressed by Wesley, laboring for others will be the natural and joyous course of each day. "Thanks be to God, the first thing I felt today was a fear of pride, and desire of love" (*Journal,* vol. I, p. 113).

---

1. John Telford, *Charles Wesley* (London: Epworth, 1927) p. 14.

18

Do We Care about God's Creation?

O Lord, how manifold are thy works!
In wisdom hast thou made them all;
the earth is full of thy creatures.
Yonder is the sea, great and wide,
which teems with things innumerable,
living things both small and great.
There go the ships,
and Leviathan which thou didst
form to sport in it.

These all look to thee,
to give them their food in due season.
When thou givest to them, they gather it up;
when thou openest thy hand,
they are filled with good things.
When thou hidest thy face, they are dismayed;
when thou takest away their breath, they die
and return to their dust.
When thou sendest forth thy Spirit, they are created;
and thou renewest the face of the ground.

—Psalm 104:24–30, RSV

Author of every work divine,
Who dost through both creations shine,
The God of nature and of grace!
Thy glorious steps in all we see,
And wisdom attribute to thee,
And power, and majesty, and praise.

Thou dost create the earth anew,
(Its Maker and Preserver too,)
By thine almighty arm sustain:
Nature perceives thy secret force,
And still holds on her even course,
And owns thy providential reign.

Thou art the Universal Soul,
The Plastic Power that fills the whole,
  And governs earth, air, sea, and sky:
The creatures all thy breath receive;
And who, by thy inspiring, live,
  Without thy inspiration, die.

—*Hymns of Petition and Thanksgiving* (1746)

Without question the earth has been sacrificed to an emphasis on human redemption, be it religious or secular. The salvation of one soul or many at all costs *and* the "reclaiming" of humankind through "civilized industrialization" have both permitted the rape of God's earth. Now nature and its creatures, including human beings, face destruction. Streams, rivers, oceans, forests, plant and animal life are threatened by technological "progress," which has brought with it a host of new human diseases that bring premature death and sickness to people daily. God's creation is under attack.

Wesley affirms the spirit of scripture that God shines "through both creations": the world of nature and humankind. God's wisdom, power, and majesty are seen in *all* creation, not just in human beings.

How often Christians hail the importance of persons becoming new creations in Christ without having a like concern for God's new creation of the earth. We are to be a part of that, too!

Nature perceives thy secret force,
And still holds on her even course.

There is a divine wisdom in nature that perceives when leaves turn multi-colored and fall, when grass turns green after the winter, when salmon spawn, when bears hibernate. On and on nature perceives the secret force. Unfortunately, human beings can thwart such perception and the rhythm of nature by exploiting nature's resources and creating natural and chemical imbalances which threaten all life. Wesley bids us, like nature, to own God's providential reign and secret force in the spirit of Psalm 104.

In an age utilizing plastic power to venture beyond this planet and others, we turn to Wesley's verse of over two hundred years ago and find him addressing God as "the Plastic Power that fills the whole." In a nuclear age when plastic power has been produced in almost unimaginable proportions, Wesley calls us back to the scripture with the words: "The creatures *all* thy breath receive."

All creation has life from God. Plants and animals receive God's *nephesh* and are alive. Some English translations have misleadingly translated this Hebrew word in Genesis 2:7 "soul," but *nephesh* is the "life principle" which distinguishes the living from the dead. According to the scriptures, in God's creation plants as well as animals have *nephesh*. Both have God-given life. Interestingly, nature, its plants and animals, somehow perceives the divine "secret force" in creation and submits to its cycle of renewal. Human beings, however, often devise means of exerting their own force against the secret force of God. Nature has not been created to satisfy their whims but for the sustenance and glory of God's creation. Nonetheless, over the centuries men and women, God's creations, have exploited nature for their own advantage, forgetting that the whole of creation is embued with the creative spirit of God. Furthermore, the Christian religious community has placed a premium on human redemption and often has not heard the rest of creation groan and wail for salvation and renewal.

Veni creator spiritus, come Creator Spirit, is a prayerful plea not only for human beings but for all of creation. Indeed, to live by the inspiration of this Spirit is life, but not at the expense of the rest of God's creation. We must live by the Spirit with a concern for God's renewal of all creation.

When thou sendest forth thy Spirit, they are created;
and thou renewest the face of the ground.

19

Can There Be Peace on Earth?

Hark! The herald-angels sing
Glory to the new-born King,
Peace on earth, and mercy mild,
God and sinners reconciled.
Joyful, all ye nations rise,
Join the triumph of the skies;
With angelic host proclaim:
"Christ is born in Bethlehem."

Christ, by highest heaven adored,
Christ, the everlasting Lord,
Late in time behold him come,
Offspring of a virgin's womb.
Veiled in flesh the Godhead see!
Hail, the incarnate Deity!
Pleased as man with men to dwell,[1]
Jesus, our Immanuel.

Hail, the heaven-born Prince of Peace!
Hail, the Sun of Righteousness!
Light and life to all he brings,
Risen with healing in his wings.
Mild he lays his glory by,
Born that man no more may die,
Born to raise the sons of earth,[2]
Born to give them second birth.

—*Hymns and Sacred Poems* (1739)

Unquestionably this hymn is one of Wesley's best known and loved throughout the English-speaking world. It is traditionally sung to a melody by the German composer Felix Mendelssohn-Bartholdy. How appropriate, since a German branch of Christendom, namely, the Moravians, had such a profound influence on Wesley's inner spiritual growth! This international connection is most fitting to a hymn which is an outcry for peace around the world and is one of Wesley's greatest legacies to people everywhere. "Hark! The herald-angels sing" is, in the truest sense, the song which he sang throughout his life and ministry.

Eighteenth-century England was a time of unrest, war, and injustice. This poem was born out of the crises, conflicts, violence, and oppression of the day and is still timely. It will never be out of date as long as there is no peace on earth.

> When nations rage with hatred and war, and innocent people are slaughtered for no cause; when humans terrorize one another in body and spirit and the clamor from the streets is but a massive cry of despair and groans of hunger; when there appears no reason for a child to be born to endure the insensibility of life; when it seems that all *is* lost and there is no hope; *there is still a song to be sung, a song which unites the music in every soul.*[3]

Hark! The herald-angels sing
Glory to the new-born King,
Peace on earth, and mercy mild,
God and sinners reconciled.

Let us pray daily two lines from a stanza of this hymn often not included in hymnbooks.

Come, Desire of nations, come,
Fix in us thy humble home.

---

1. Erik Routley, *Rejoice in the Lord, op. cit.*, Nr. 196 suggests: "pleased in flesh with us to dwell."
2. *Ibid.*, "born that we no more may die,
born to raise us from the earth."
3. S T Kimbrough, Jr., *Sweet Singer,* a musical about Charles Wesley, copyright by author (1985) p. 25, used by permission.

How Does Love for Others Grow?

Love divine, all loves excelling
  Joy of heaven, to earth come down;
Fix in us thy humble dwelling,
  All thy faithful mercies crown:
Jesus, thou art all compassion,
  Pure, unbounded love thou art;
Visit us with thy salvation,
  Enter every trembling heart.

Breathe, O breathe thy loving Spirit
  Into every troubled breast,
Let us all in thee inherit,
  Let us find that second rest:
Take away our bent to sinning,
  Alpha and Omega be
End of faith as its beginning,
  Set our hearts at liberty.

Come, almighty to deliver,
  Let us all thy grace receive;
Suddenly return, and never,
  Never more thy temples leave:
Thee we would be always blessing,
  Serve thee as thy hosts above,
Pray, and praise thee, without ceasing,
  Glory in thy perfect love.

Finish then thy new creation,
  Pure and spotless let us be;
Let us see thy great salvation,
  Perfectly restored in thee;
Changed from glory into glory,
  Till in heaven we take our place,
Till we cast our crowns before thee,
  Lost in wonder, love, and praise.

—*Redemption Hymns* (1747)

Shortly before they married (February, 1749), Charles Wesley wrote to his bride-to-be, Sally Gwynne:

> You have heard me acknowledge that at first sight "My soul seemed pleased to take acquaintance with thee." And never have I found such a nearness to any fellow-creature as to you. O that it may bring us nearer and nearer to God, till we are both swallowed up in the immensity of His love![1]

Above all else Wesley wanted to be "swallowed up" in God's love, for all loves begin, end, and are fulfilled in that love. With this confidence he wrote one of the most meaningful and eloquent prayers for a love-filled life ever written, "Love divine, all loves excelling."

If we want to grow in love, this prayer hymn should be our daily guide. It directs us how to pray and grow in God's love.

Acknowledge God as the source of unbounded, limitless love (stanza one). Pray to be the dwelling-place of God's love; pray also for the indwelling of Christ.

Pray in the plural, not just in the singular (stanza two). Pray that the Holy Spirit will enter the lives of *others* also so that every troubled breast will be set at liberty. Through the power of the Holy Spirit we can be freed from the desire to do what is wrong and set free to love.

Pray for the reception of God's grace (stanza three) which enables us to live the self-giving love expressed in Jesus Christ. When we receive God's grace, we recognize that God does for us what we cannot do for ourselves: God reclaims our sinful lives and makes them new through Christ. When we live renewed lives, we begin to learn what it means to mature in love. Love takes priority over everything in our lives. There is no compromise.

Pray to be created new (stanza four) and to continue in the creative process toward maturity in love. Wesley understood that to finish the new creation means lifelong spiritual growth. The ongoing process is defined by the word *till,* which designates the time between what has been and what will be, between *no longer* and *not yet.* He anticipates the time when we shall meet God in glory and be matured, new creatures in God's perfect love. We do not have to wait, however, for a "heavenly reward" to mature in love. In Christ we are new creations now. The great salvation perfectly restored in heaven is the fulfillment of the salvation we receive on earth.

As followers of Christ who want to grow in love, what is important is the continuing creative process within us. There is no one who does not need to grow in love. If we use the guidelines of this hymn for our prayer life, we will live lives that are "lost in wonder, love, and praise."

---

1. Frank Baker, *Charles Wesley as Revealed by His Letters, op. cit.,* p. 55.

21

Do We Give Unbelievers a Chance?

Now these Jews were more noble than those in Thessalonica, for they received the word with all eagerness, examining the scriptures daily to see if these things were so. Many of them therefore believed, with not a few Greek women of high standing as well as men.

—Acts 17:11–12, RSV

Can we in unbelievers find
That noble readiness of mind
To hear, investigate, and prove
The truth of Jesu's pardoning Love?
Yes, Lord; through thy preventing grace,
There are who cordially embrace
The joyful news of sin forgiven,
With God by grace sent down from heaven.

—*Scripture Hymns,* 1762

How readily the world often is divided into "believers" and "unbelievers." And it is easy for believers to view themselves as much better off than those who have not yet believed. These verses from Acts remind us that unbelievers have a nobility all their own which may prepare them to receive God's word with an open mind. Wesley affirms the divine purpose which shrouds unbelievers. We find an example of this in the Old Testament, when the prophet Isaiah calls the Median King Cyrus a messiah. Cyrus was neither an Israelite nor a follower of their God. He decreed that the Israelites in Babylonian exile could return to their homeland, and Isaiah viewed him as "anointed," a messiah, the same name used for Jesus.

The believing community can build bridges to those who do not believe by fostering a spirit of free inquiry affirmed by scripture. There are no exclusive rights to God's word. Our attitudes, however, may in fact exclude others from the gospel. The scripture pleads: Keep an open mind toward everyone.

Wesley continues:

> What then are they that dare forbid
> The unconvinced thy Book to read,
> Who take the sacred key away,
> Damp their desire to search and pray,
> Conceal thy records from their view;
> "The Scriptures were not wrote for you:
> Accept your more unerring guide,
> The Church, the Catholics—the Bride!"

Will another believe because we are open-minded?

Is the Church Really for Everyone?

O for a thousand tongues to sing
  My great Redeemer's praise!
The glories of my God and King,
  The triumphs of his grace.

My gracious Master and my God,
  Assist me to proclaim,
To spread through all the earth abroad
  The honors of thy name.

Jesus the name that charms our fears,
  That bids our sorrows cease;
'Tis music in the sinner's ears,
  'Tis life, and health, and peace.

He breaks the power of cancelled sin,
  He sets the prisoner free:
His blood can make the foulest clean;
  His blood availed for me.

He speaks; and listening to his voice,
  New life the dead receive,
The mournful, broken hearts rejoice,
  The humble poor believe.

Hear him ye deaf, his praise ye dumb
  Your loosened tongues employ,
Ye blind, behold your Savior come,
  And leap, ye lame, for joy.

—*Hymns and Sacred Poems* (1740)

The inspiration for this hymn came from the words of the Moravian Christian Peter Boehler, whom Charles Wesley taught English. Boehler is reported to have said to Wesley that if he had a thousand tongues he would use them all to praise God. Wesley had heard Christians worship in other tongues. He remembered throughout his life the inspirational German hymns sung by the Moravians on board the ship *Simmonds* on his voyage to America. He had read the fathers of the church in Latin and the New Testament in Greek. He and his brother John even learned to converse in Latin. Charles Wesley knew there were many tongues with which to praise God, and it is not surprising that the impetus for this great hymn, which was written for the anniversary day of one's conversion, should come from someone whose mother tongue was other than English and who was extremely influential in Wesley's own quest for authentic faith.

The hymn originally had eighteen stanzas, although most hymnbooks usually include only those quoted here, which are stanzas seven through twelve. The first six tell of a powerful life transforming experience. For example, stanza five:

I felt my Lord's atoning blood
  Close to my soul applied;
Me, *me* he loved the son of God
  For *me,* for *me* He died!

The familiar stanzas on page 87 are a universal appeal to praise God. Two stanzas often omitted fuse praise with mission and remind us of the inclusiveness of the gospel:

Harlots, and publicans, and thieves
  In holy triumph join!
Saved is the sinner that believes
  From crimes as great as mine.

Murderers, and all ye hellish crew,
  Ye sons of lust and pride,
Believe the Savior died for you,
  For me the Savior died.

How many churches consciously seek out prostitutes, thieves, criminals of all sorts, murderers, and hell raisers? Yet, Jesus sought them.

How many churches seek to make the following affirmation a reality?

> Hear him ye deaf, his praise ye dumb
>   Your loosened tongues employ,
> Ye blind, behold your Savior come,
>   And leap, ye lame, for joy.

How many churches make their worship experiences accessible to the deaf, blind, and lame? Are sign language, hearing aids, braille, ramps, lifts, wheelchairs, and vehicles with hydraulic lifts available to those in need? Are there classes for persons with learning disabilities? If not, the church is saying to persons with related problems, "You are not welcome to participate in our worship and church program." Wesley's metaphors of impairment do emphasize inclusive ministry, but they point to a deeper reality; when our tongues are not loosed to praise God and we do not acknowledge that the Savior has come, we are impaired.

"O for a thousand tongues to sing" stresses not only the need for a global outcry of praise to God but calls the church and individual Christians to fulfill their mission: praise *and* reach out to all.

23

What Is True Freedom?

Spirit of faith, come down on me,
For where thou art is liberty;
Thy presence looses all my bands,
And melts the fetters from my hands,
Consumes like flax the cords of sin,
And burns up all my foes within.

—*Scripture Hymns* (1762)

Some years ago my youngest son and I went to a summer camp in Czechoslovakia which was attended by Christians from over twenty countries. During our first meeting we were divided into groups of three and told to discuss three words: *faith, hope,* and *freedom.* In my group was a young married man from the host country and a soldier in its army. I recall that when we came to the word *freedom,* I asked him what freedom(s) he felt had been taken from him by the Russian military domination of his country. His reply was direct, immediate, and convincing. "None at all," he said, "because when you have the inner freedom of God's Spirit, no one can take away your freedom. They can restrict your mobility, but they cannot take away your freedom because it is eternally yours within." He was living fulfillment of Wesley's prayer:

Spirit of faith, come down on me,
For where thou art is liberty.

Although he could not travel to any destination he might choose, the Spirit of faith had descended upon him to dwell within and he was free indeed! No military presence from any country of the world could take away that freedom.

When the Spirit of God comes to dwell in us by faith in the gift of love expressed in Jesus Christ (God among us in life, ministry, death, and resurrection), we are liberated from the tyranny of others and ourselves. No matter what our situation, it is God's *presence* in us which shatters all external and internal shackles or chains which bind us. This is why the church lives on in times of persecution and oppression. The tyranny of governments and dictators is no match for the Spirit of faith alive and dynamic in the lives of all who make up the church, the body of Christ.

The Spirit of faith frees us likewise from the tyranny of ourselves. We can be ruled inwardly by many forces: greed, hate, lust, hunger for power, wealth, success. But when we allow God through the Spirit of faith to be our indwelling power, these burning desires are consumed by the flame of love which overtakes us as rapidly as flax vanishes in a fire.

Christians will struggle to free all people because of their commitment to the reign of God's justice on earth; nonetheless, they know that if they are not free within—if the Spirit of faith has not come down on them—they shall never be free, even if liberated from some worldly bondage.

24

Can There Be an End to Bloodshed?

Spirit of faith, come down,
Reveal the things of God,
And make to us the Godhead known,
And witness with the blood:
'Tis thine the blood to apply,
And give us eyes to see,
Who did for every sinner die
Hath surely died for me.

No one can truly say
That Jesus is the Lord
Unless thou take the veil away,
And breathe the living word;
Then, only then, we feel
Our interest in his blood,
And cry with joy unspeakable,
Thou art my Lord, my God!

O that the world might know
The all-atoning Lamb!
Spirit of faith, descend, and show
The virtue of his name;
The grace which all may find,
The saving power impart,
And testify to humankind,
And speak in every heart!

Inspire the living faith
(Which whosoe'er receives,
The witness in himself he hath,
And consciously believes),
The faith that conquers all,
And doth the mountain move,
And saves whoe'er on Jesus call,
And perfects them in love.

—*Hymns of Petition and Thanksgiving* (1746)

In this hymn Wesley lays down four distinct needs of human beings in relation to the gift of the Holy Spirit: revelation, recognition, reclamation, and regeneration.

Stanza one is a prayer for revelation, a prayer to have our inner eyes opened to see the "things of God" more clearly; namely, knowing the Godhead (who God is) and God's activity (what God does). It may seem rather strange that Wesley prays for the Spirit to "witness with the blood." History tells us, however, that this is a human preoccupation. People in every age have tried to witness to some point, cause, or way of life by spilling the blood of others. Life today is haunted by terrorists representing political, national, and religious interests. Those people seek to further their interests by "applying blood," that is, by taking the lives of others, even children and infants. Such deaths are viewed by the perpetrators as effectual and purifying for their causes. God's Spirit reveals to those who will hear the meaning of Christ's death, how the witness of his blood was for all people so that they might understand how much God loves them and seek to live together in the spirit of that love.

Stanza two is a prayer for the personal recognition: "Thou art my Lord, my God!" The corporate and communal recognition of the lordship of Christ begins with the individual. This transpires when the veil between the human and divine is taken away and one breathes the living Word. That is reminiscent of Wesley's prayer in the hymn, "Love divine, all loves excelling":

> Breathe, O breathe thy loving Spirit
> Into every troubled breast.

It is the loving Spirit, the living Word, which evokes an interest in the blood of Christ. One is filled with the Spirit of love and sees the futility of all human bloodshed. That indeed is worthy of human interest! Christ's sacrifice brings the reign of love on earth "because God's love has been poured into our hearts through the Holy Spirit which has been given to us" (Romans 5:5, RSV).

Stanza three is a prayer for the universal reclamation of humankind. As definitive as Wesley is in stanza two about personal confession of Christ's lordship, this stanza is wholly inclusive in its language as he pleads for the descent of the Spirit upon all humankind.

> O that the *world* might know
> The *all*-atoning Lamb!
> . . . .
>
> The grace which *all* may find,
> . . . .
>
> And speak in *every* heart!

Eighteenth-century England was plagued with religious disunity. There were divisions such as the Papists, Dissenters, Calvinists and many more. Furthermore Wesley saw a schism developing between the Methodist Societies and the Church of England. There were political divisions as well—those who were loyal to the crown and others who favored a Pretender to the throne. Human loyalties are willing to sacrifice others to their causes and breed enmity. Wesley cries out that the course of human history can be changed only by reclaiming broken humankind through the descent of the Spirit of love upon *every* heart—through a universal awareness that it is no longer necessary to live by the false notion that others must be sacrificed to a human cause. God's sacrifice of the Son, Jesus, has shown us the virtue of his name which is "Salvation" and given us a pattern for living in harmony: give of self in love for others and God.

Stanza four is a prayer for regeneration. The faith which moves mountains and gives life a new beginning is one which perfects in love those who call on the name of Jesus. The verb *perfects* is at the heart of redemption and social harmony, for it reflects the process of maturing in love as followers of Jesus. "O that the world might know" that it can grow in love and peace instead of hatred and war. Such a worldwide regeneration, new birth, or new beginning is the hope of the descent of the Spirit of love which God pours into our hearts. The shedding of Christ's blood is the sign and seal of this Spirit which can so fill human hearts with love that there will be no more bloodshed on earth.

25

Can People Be United?

I will give them one heart and one way, that they may fear me forever.

—Jeremiah 32:39, RSV

No, they cry, it cannot be!
Christians never will agree.
All the world thy word deny;
Yet we on the truth rely,
Sure, in that appointed day,
Thou wilt give us all one way.
Show us each to other joined,
One in heart, and one in mind.

Hasten then the general peace,
Bid thy people's discord cease;
All united in thy Name,
Let us think and speak the same.
Then the world shall know and own
The Divine hath made us one;
Thee their Lord with us embrace
Sing thine everlasting praise.

—*Scripture Hymns* (1762)

The promise of one unified heart and a singular path of life was not fulfilled for God's people in Jeremiah's time, nor during Wesley's eighteenth-century England. And we still await its realization in our day. God, who does not flag in faithfulness to the covenants and promises made throughout scripture, is ever ready to fulfill this ancient promise. It remains unfulfilled because Christians themselves have decided that they never will agree. This is a blatant repudiation of God's word and a signal to the world that Christians deny its validity by their fragmented community.

Wesley knew what it meant to experience such fragmentation firsthand. On one occasion he was refused

Holy Communion at Temple Church and recorded the incident in his journal.

> The Clerk came to me, and said, "Mr. Beacher bids you go away, for he will not give you the sacrament." I went to the vestry-door, and mildly desired Mr. Beacher to admit me. He asked, "Are you of this parish?" I answered, "Sir, you *see* I am a Clergyman." Dropping his first pretence, he charged me with rebellion in expounding the Scriptures without authority; and said in express words, "I repel you from the sacrament." I replied, "I cite you to answer this before Jesus Christ at the day of judgment." This enraged him above measure. He called out, *"Here, take away this man!"*...but I saved them the trouble...and quietly retired.
>
> —*Journal,* vol. I, p. 246

Hasten then the day of peace,
Bid thy people's discord cease.

These lines are not pious platitudes of a clergyman comfortably entrenched in denominationalism yet somehow compelled to speak of things beyond realization in this world. No! They are the agonizing outcry of Wesley's soul, for he had grasped that only if Christians *personify* oneness will others know God has united them. Such unity will bring them to God. In other words, the unity of Christians *is* evangelism!

V

Ourselves

Oh, what am I if left to myself?
But I can do and suffer
all things
through Christ strengthening me.

Charles Wesley

26

How Do We Overcome Trials and Persecution?

Ye servants of God, your Master proclaim,
And publish abroad his wonderful name;
The name all-victorious of Jesus extol;
His kingdom is glorious and rules over all.

The waves of the sea have lift up their voice,
Sore troubled that we in Jesus rejoice;
The floods they are roaring, but Jesus is here,
While we are adoring, he always is near.

Men, devils engage, the billows arise,
And horribly rage, and threaten the skies:
Their fury shall never our steadfastness shock,
The weakest believer is built on a rock.

God ruleth on high, almighty to save;
And still he is nigh, his presence we have;
The great congregation his triumph shall sing,
Ascribing salvation to Jesus our King.

"Salvation to God who sits on the throne!"
Let all cry aloud and honor the Son!
Our praises of Jesus the angels proclaim,
Fall down on their faces, and worship the Lamb.

Then let us adore, and give him his right:
All glory and power, all wisdom and might,
All honor and blessing, with angels above
And thanks never ceasing, and infinite love.

—*Hymns for Times of Trouble and Persecution* (1744)

Since stanzas two and three of this hymn are omitted in most hymnbooks, the life situation out of which the hymn was born is easily overlooked. Charles knew the agony of severe persecution and the necessity of standing firm in the faith against all opposition. The 1740s were extremely troubled times, filled with suspicion of those averred to be disloyal to the Crown and to favor a Pretender to the throne of England. Many seized the opportunity to oppose the followers of the Wesleys who were slandered and violently attacked by unruly mobs on numerous occasions. Charles himself was labelled a rogue, rascal, villain, pickpocket and even the representative of a Pretender to the throne, whom some thought to be his brother John disguised as a priest. Although the Wesleys persistently maintained their loyalty to the Crown, opposition mounted. It is miraculous that they were not killed by the raging mobs. At Walsal, John was dragged by the hair from the steps of the cross down the main street, and Charles was attacked while preaching from the market steps.

"Ye servants of God" is a Christian pledge of allegiance to God for the faithful who serve One who is greater than all kings. God rules above all, and there are no Pretenders with any claims whatsoever to the throne upon which the Author of salvation sits.

Any struggle for an earthly crown involves conflicts over who shall have the right, glory, power, wisdom, might, honor, and blessing ascribed to a monarch's throne. Wesley ascribes all these to God, and his hymn leaves no doubt that though he may have been loyal to the Crown of England, his ultimate allegiance was to God. The following account of an event at Sheffield on May 25, 1743 from his *Journal* reveals this allegiance:

> At six I went to the Society-house, next door to our brother Bennet's. Hell from beneath was moved to oppose us. As soon as I was in the desk with David Taylor, the floods began to lift up their voice. An officer (Ensign Garden) contradicted and blasphemed. I took no notice of him, and sang on. The stones flew thick, hitting the desk and people. To save them and the house, I gave notice I should preach out, and look the enemy in the face.
>
> The whole army of aliens followed me. The Captain laid hold on me, and began reviling. I gave him for answer, "A Word in season; or, Advice to a Soldier;"

> then prayed, particularly for His Majesty King George, and preached the gospel with much contention. The stones often struck me in the face. After the sermon I prayed for sinners, as servants of their master, the devil; upon which the Captain ran at me with great fury, threatening revenge for my abusing, as he called it, "the King his master." He forced his way through the brethren, drew his sword, and presented it to my breast. My breast was immediately steeled. I threw it open, and, fixing mine eye on his, smiled in his face, and calmly said, "I fear God, and honor the King." His countenance fell in a moment, he fetched a deep sigh, put up his sword, and quietly left the place.
>
> —*Journal,* vol. I, p. 309

We live in an age filled with mobs and rioting, and followers of Jesus are called upon anew to stand firm in their faith as champions of "infinite love." Amid political, economic, and social injustices, Christians around the world are beckoned to turn the cries of agony and hatred into resounding praises of God. The love of God in Jesus is so transforming that it can change discriminatory laws, rectify the exploitation of the poor by the rich, provide shelter for the homeless and food for the hungry. And on it goes. Injustices fall before God's love!

"Ye servants of God" is an eighteenth-century cry of the soul against oppression and persecution not unlike the twentieth-century outcry against injustice in the song "We Shall Overcome." It is through faith that we have the power to overcome. Charles Wesley illustrated this not only with his pen but with his life. God calls us to do the same.

What Are We Really Like?

Gentle Jesus, meek and mild,
Look upon a little child,
Pity my simplicity,
Suffer me to come to thee.

Fain I would be as thou art;
Give me thy obedient heart;
Thou art pitiful and kind;
Let me have thy loving mind.

Let me above all fulfill
God my heavenly Father's will;
Never God's good Spirit grieve,
Only to God's glory live.

Loving Jesus, gentle Lamb,
In thy gracious hands I am;
Make me, Savior, what thou art;
Live thyself within my heart.

I shall then show forth thy praise,
Serve thee all my happy days;
Then the world shall always see
Christ, the holy child, in me.

—*Hymns and Sacred Poems* (1742)

All of us have been children. Perhaps there are times when we long to return to our childhood, that is, to recapture those aspects of being a child which affirm life at its best and as God intended it to be. Charles Wesley once said, "Be a little child yourself and a child will be led by you into all that is right."[1] He and his wife, Sally, had eight children, but only three of them survived the plagues of infancy and childhood: Charles, Jr., Sally, and Samuel. Therefore, the inner yearnings expressed in the above poem grew not only out of his own experience as a child but also out of those of his children with all of the accompanying anguish of suffering and death. How could one long to be a child when one had lived on the brink of poverty and seen his own children suffer and die from illnesses not yet controlled in the eighteenth century?

Being a child means maintaining our simplicity (stanza one). Children have an ability to cut through the complexities of life in what they say and do. They often express and demonstrate insight free of the machinery of logic and reasoning. As we sat at the breakfast table one morning with our four small sons, the three youngest, ages three, four and five, spread marmalade on their faces, the table, the floor, and a little on the toast. The parental edict was issued sternly: "People do not eat like that!" The four-year-old calmly replied, "But we're not people; we're children." We saw in him the person he should become, but he saw himself as he was—a child. With those simple words I realized as never before the importance of accepting people as they are and not as I want them to be.

Being a child means maintaining an obedient heart and a loving mind (stanza two). Parents and guardians of children expect children to obey them, and they establish rules for behavior. Our relationship to God is like that. God is the divine parent with expectations of behavior for us, the children of creation. God has established rules which we are to observe. Note, however, we do not keep them for the sake of the rules. The obedient heart and the loving mind go together. We keep them out of love for God, others, and the world God has made. The loving mind of children gives them an ability to forgive, forget, and accept others as they are. According to the scriptures, these are godlike qualities—ones which adults unfortunately often leave behind with their childhood.

Being a child means maintaining the desire to fulfill God's will (stanza three). Children do not always find it easy to do what their parents want. As children, however, they usually fulfill the will of their parents because their parents have the authority to expect the same. As we grow to adulthood, God's expectation of our fulfillment of divine will does not diminish. But we often allow our wills to take precedence over God's will. For example, God wills life, justice, peace, and love for all people, yet we live in a world that does not fulfill those divine expectations. As children of creation we are to fulfill the desires of the Parent of all parents, God the Creator.

Being a child means maintaining Christ in our hearts, God's praise on our lips, and service to God in all we do (stanzas four and five). Being a Christian means being like a child. Perhaps we can learn more about being Christians and living the faith from children than we have ever imagined. This may have motivated Wesley to write in his *Journal* these words: "I was glad to hear of one of our English brethren, lately brought back by a little child, who told his father something...and disturbed him, so that he could not sleep at night, since they left off family prayer" (*Journal,* vol. I, p. 351).

We cannot return to our childhood, but we can be a child in spirit throughout our lives. We can pray daily:

> God, I want to be a child always. Give me an obedient heart, a loving mind, and the desire to do what you want for me, others, and the world you made. Live in my heart and make me what Jesus is—*love*—and I will serve you every day I live. In the name of your Holy Child. *Amen.*

---

1. John Telford, *Charles Wesley, op. cit.,* p. 44.

What Is Our Outlook on Life?

Rejoice, the Lord is King!
Your Lord and King adore;
Mortals, give thanks, and sing,
And triumph evermore:

Lift up your heart, lift up your voice;
Rejoice! Again I say: Rejoice!

Jesus the Savior reigns,
The God of truth and love;
When he had purged our stains,
He took his seat above:

His kingdom cannot fail,
He rules o'er earth and heaven;
The keys of death and hell
Are to our Jesus given:

He sits at God's right hand
Till all his foes submit,
And bow to his command,
And fall beneath his feet:

Rejoice in glorious hope;
Jesus the Judge shall come
And take his servants up
To their eternal home:

We soon shall hear the archangel's voice;
The trump of God shall sound: Rejoice!

—*Hymns for our Lord's Resurrection* (1746)

As an airport bus transporting passengers from one terminal to another made its rounds, one passenger who boarded at the first stop and was riding to the last noticed something interesting taking place. Almost all who boarded were unpleasant and complaining about their trip, airline services, delays, and the like. With every announcement of the next terminal, the bus driver prefaced the name of the stop by saying, "Hello, folks! This is your happy bus driver telling you how fortunate you are to be able to travel and to get on and off this bus. The next stop is . . ." At the last stop there was not an unpleasant person on the bus. The driver had changed everyone's unhappiness into joy. Happiness breeds happiness.

The hallmark of Christian behavior is joy. Christian life is the exclamation of joy: "Rejoice! Again I say: Rejoice!" The first four verses of Wesley's hymn resound with the refrain:

> Lift up your hearts, lift up your voice:
> Rejoice! Again I say: Rejoice!
> Life up your hearts, life up your voice:
> Rejoice! Again I say: Rejoice!

The first and last word of the hymn is "Rejoice!" Do not be low-spirited, brokenhearted, downtrodden, and a complainer throughout life! Be joyous! Joy breeds joy!

Wesley summarizes the reasons why Christians should rejoice. The Lord is King. The Bible often speaks of God as King, the One who reigns over creation. Psalm 24:8 repeats:

> Who is the King of glory?
> The LORD, strong and mighty,
> the LORD, mighty in battle! (RSV)

The Revelation to John (11:15) declares, "The kingdom of the world has become the kingdom of our Lord and of his Christ, and he shall reign for ever and ever" (RSV). The Christian understands that God—not earthly rulers—is at the helm of existence.

Jesus the Savior reigns. Jesus' rule is not one of deception and hatred but one of truth and love. As we look at world diplomacy and the secret intelligence agencies of nations worldwide, we see clearly that governments and their leaders have not yet fully grasped the reign of One who puts all relationships on the basis of truth and love. That is the world's hope!

His kingdom cannot fail. History often is written by reviewing the rise and fall of great empires such as those of Egypt, Greece, and Rome. While earthly kingdoms rise and fall, God's kingdom of earth *and* heaven endures, for it is built upon truth and love. Jesus has shown us in his death and resurrection that even death is turned into triumph and victory in God's realm.

Jesus the Judge shall come. There is life and hope which are larger than earthly existence. God's creative process does not end with physical death but works out its purpose in earth and heaven; those who serve God will not have served in vain. Their destiny will be judged by the truth and love of Jesus which endures forever.

Christians have cause to rejoice indeed! When we are despondent and despairing: Rejoice! When others about us are unpleasant and depressed: Rejoice! Rejoicing breeds rejoicing! Today give someone's heart a change of mood. Rejoice!

How Do We Deal with Sickness?

And live I yet by power divine?
  And have I still my course to run?
Again brought back in its decline
  The shadow of my parting sun?

Wond'ring I ask, is this the breast
  Struggling so late and torn with pain!
The eyes that upward looked for rest,
  And dropped their weary lids again!

My feeble flesh refused to bear
  Its strong redoubled agonies:
When mercy heard my speechless prayer,
  And saw me faintly gasp for ease.

The fever turned its backward course,
  Arrested by Almighty power;
Sudden expired its fiery force,
  And anguish gnawed my side no more.

God of my life, what just return
  Can sinful dust and ashes give?
I only live my sin to mourn,
  To love my God I only live.

Be all my added life employed
  Thy image in my soul to see:
Fill with thyself the mighty void;
  Enlarge my heart to compass thee!

Prepare and then possess my heart,
  O take me, seize me from above:
Thee do I love, for God thou art;
  Thee do I feel, for God is love.

—*Hymns and Sacred Poems* (1739)

Charles Wesley did not always enjoy good health. More than once he recovered from what might have been a fatal illness. Any of us who have faced grave sickness and pain, who have been brought back from what seemed certain death, know what it means to ask ourselves: "And have I still my course to run?" Is everything not at an end? Do I really have a new lease on life? Yet, Wesley prefaces this question with another: "And live I yet by power divine?"

It is not merely a question of whether we have the power to go on but whether we go on in God's strength. Illnesses have tremendous psychological power, and sometimes when sick we make well-meaning but wrongheaded promises to ourselves and God—if we can just get well. "God, if you will spare me, I will..." "If I make it, I will never again..." Indeed, an illness may shock us into awareness and reality that set our lives on the proper course after recovery. But whether we die or live, we may do so in God's strength, by the "power divine."

Recovery brings with it a sense of wonder and awe that our fevered, weak bodies have been restored to health and wholeness. When we have endured tremendous pain and longed for it to cease, we know its subsiding is mercy and grace in action. One of my sons once lay in a hospital bed for weeks at the threshold of death. On one occasion, when his pain and bodily condition were gravest, he said to me, "I look forward to the time when I can look back on all this and say, 'I made it.'" About a year later after his amazing recovery, he said, "Dad, you know I'm a walking miracle!" Hold fast to the sense of wonder after recovery and live by the power divine!

Recovery brings with it a sense that we have a debt to pay for being spared. Although we are accustomed to incurring medical debts during illnesses, our only debt to God upon recovery is love.

God of my life, what just return
  Can sinful dust and ashes give?
I only live my sin to mourn
  To love my God I only live.

Recovery brings with it lengthened life and the choice of what we shall do with it. Wesley says the choice which governs all others is the decision to be filled with God and God's love. There is one type of enlarged heart which is healthy, the one enlarged to encompass God: "Enlarge my heart to compass thee." There is one type of seizure which is healthy, the seizure of love:

> Prepare and then possess my heart
> O take me, seize me from above:
> Thee do I love, for God thou art;
> Thee do I feel, for God is love.

Recovery brings with it the renewed opportunity to love God and to be the embodiment of love. That is what it means to live by the power divine.

30

Are We Bigots?

There is no fear of God at all in this place, and they will kill me because of my wife.

—Genesis 20:11, RSV

Forgive my partial selfishness,
  My rash, censorious thought,
"Among this people, in this place,
  Surely the Lord is not!
If strangers to my sect and name,
  Strangers they are to thee:
God is not feared, except by them
  Who know and honor me."

—*Scripture Hymns* (1762)

The words of Genesis 20:11 are Abraham's explanation to King Abimelech as to why he had deceived the king in saying that his wife, Sarah, was his sister. Trusting Abraham's word, Abimelech had taken Sarah for himself. How wrong and bigoted Abraham was! God *was* in that place and appeared to Abimelech in a dream and revealed the truth about Sarah. The next morning the king was obedient to God's command and returned her to her husband, Abraham.

The apostle Paul was aware of similar bigotry in the early church when he wrote to the Christians at Corinth and reproached them for their divisions into followers of Paul, Apollos, Cephas, and Christ (1 Corinthians 1:12–13). They had become certain that God was to be found only by following their specific leader.

The fragmented nature of global Christianity with its multiple and ever-growing denominations and sects reminds us that we and our ancestors in the faith are guilty of selfishness and rash, censorious thought.

The Church of the Holy Sepulchre in Jerusalem, a symbol of Christianity to the world for centuries, at times has symbolized more bigotry and hate than it has unity and love. It is owned by a number of churches whose relationships have not always been harmonious. Once, they deteriorated to such a point that a monk was murdered for stepping over the boundary of his church's section of the building. So difficult were the continuing controversies that the mayor of Jerusalem appointed a Moslem to be the doorkeeper and holder of the key, since the various churches could not even agree on when to open the door.

No one, no group, no place has a monopoly on faith or God, but it is easy to fall prey to the opinion that we are right and others are wrong. The scripture warns us that God is in the place we least suspect, and Wesley has provided us with the appropriate prayer of forgiveness for individuals and for the church. Would that it were prayed at the beginning of all denominational meetings. It is a prayer worthy of memorization and constant repetition in private and public. It will help us to be forgiving Christians even as we have been forgiven in Christ.

Are We Saints?

If I justify myself, mine own mouth shall condemn me: if I say I am perfect, it shall also prove me perverse.

—Job 9:20, KJV

Though all the precious promises
I find fulfilled in Jesus' love,
If perfect I myself profess,
My own profession I disprove.

The purest saint that lives below
Doth his own sanctity disclaim;
The wisest owns, I nothing know,
The holiest cries, I nothing am.

—*Scripture Hymns* (1762)

Perfection is the impossible ideal for which we untiringly strive in many areas of life. Those who claim to attain it affirm their imperfection through the claim itself. Athletes may pursue perfection in their respective sports; musicians in their singing, playing, or composing; writers and speakers in their mastery of language; scientists and academicians in their specific subjects of research and experimentation. Nevertheless, there is yet a higher quest for perfection which gives all these other pursuits deeper and fuller meaning—the quest of perfection in love. This is the love personified in Jesus, which gives of self for others and pours out tenderness, understanding, healing, concern, friendship, reconciliation, and justice. It pursues and shrouds all people regardless of intellectual, social, or economic status.

Sometimes people are designated as "saintly" by the church as well as by individuals. When someone says of another, "He or she is a saint," we know it is not because such a person has claimed sainthood for himself or herself but rather has disclaimed it.

Truly great musicians know that there is no such thing as a perfect performance of a musical work because there will always be many varied and valid interpretations by diverse performers. Hence, the claim, "That was a perfect performance!" is only an illusion.

The hymn "I Sing a Song of the Saints of God" declares:

> For the saints of God are just folk like me,
> And I mean to be one too.[1]

That means all of us should mold our lives as saints, but not in the sense of thinking we can *attain* perfection. We must, however, *pursue* perfection as faithful servants of Jesus who wish to be perfect in love. Two of the great virtues of a saint are *purity* and *wisdom*. Wesley affirms biblical truth in this short poem by making clear that we are purest when we disclaim being pure and wisest when we disclaim being wise. This is the path to perfection.

---

1. Number 243, *The Hymnal* of the Protestant Episcopal Church in the USA, (New York: Church Hymnal Corporation, 1940).

32

Are We Ablaze with Love?

See how great a flame aspires,
Kindled by a spark of grace!
Jesus' love the nations fires,
Sets the kingdoms on a blaze.
To bring fire on earth he came;
Kindled in some hearts it is;
O that all might catch the flame,
All partake the glorious bliss!

—*Hymns and Sacred Poems* (1749)

There is something enchanting and terrifying about fire. It can bring us warmth and comfort or destruction and death. Most of us have played with fire as children much to the despair of our parents, guardians, and elders. How delightful, however, to sit before a fireplace to escape the shivering cold of a winter night, watching the flickering, dancing flames play about the room. Yet how horrifying to see homes and buildings melt, tumble, and be devoured by a devastating, overwhelming blaze of fire!

Charles Wesley's ministry took him to the coal miners of Staffordshire and the iron workers of Newcastle where he felt the heat and saw the fires common to such work. He knew they would understand the imagery of their own labor applied to the gospel. Hence, he wrote this hymn which includes an additional three verses. It is still up-to-date.

Every fire is begun by a spark. When the spark plugs in a motor function properly, the fuel is ignited, resulting in the needed power for motion. As Christians we, too, are involved in an ignition process, namely, kindling the flame of God's love wherever we are. The spark of grace with which Wesley indicates we are to ignite the fire is Jesus' love. This is the fire Jesus brings on earth, not the fire of bombs and destruction. But "kindled in *some* hearts it is," not in all. People and nations have not yet learned to shower their enemies with food, clothing, and medical supplies instead of napalm. Only *some* have.

As followers of Jesus, our work is unfinished. We have more fires of love to ignite: "O that *all* might catch the flame!" This excludes no one and includes everyone!

Spark a fire of love every day in the hearts and lives of others. They will catch the flames of God's love which will spread, grow, and glow. It will consume the flames of hatred and destruction.

Be ablaze with love!

Are We Forgiving?

Forgive, and ye shall be forgiven.

—Luke 6:37, KJV

Forgive my foes? it cannot be:
  My foes with cordial love embrace?
Fast bound in sin and misery,
  Unsaved, unchanged by hallowing grace,
Throughout my fallen soul I feel
With man this is impossible.

Great Searcher of the mazy heart,
  A thought from thee I would not hide
I cannot draw th'envenomed dart,
  Or quench this hell of wrath and pride,
Jesus, till I thy Spirit receive,
Thou know'st, I never can forgive.

Come, Lord, and tame the tiger's force,
  Arrest the whirlwind in my will,
Turn back the torrent's rapid course,
  And bid the headlong sun stand still,
The rock dissolve, the mountain move,
And melt my hatred into love.

Root out the wrath thou dost retain;
  And when I have my Savior's mind,
I cannot render pain for pain,
  I cannot speak a word unkind,
An angry thought I cannot know,
Or count mine injurer my foe.

—*Scripture Hymns* (1762)

Is forgiveness possible for human beings? With God's help, yes! To say we forgive glides quite easily from our lips at times, but to take our foes in our arms, embrace them, and express love and forgiveness is much more difficult. It is especially difficult in a world where people and nations constantly guard their space, where people continue to be persecuted for racial, creedal, political, and cultural backgrounds, where the industry of war provides massive global employment, and where murder, robbery, and war are the daily agenda in so much of the world. On a more personal level, people have their hometown enemies. Grudges, enmity, jealousy, and hatred devour the human sense of decency, integrity, respect, and concern for others.

Wesley understood that until we receive the Spirit of Jesus we are incapable of true forgiveness. Without that Spirit we cannot "quench this hell of wrath and pride." There is a power within us which feeds enmity and hatred between us and others. It has the force of a tiger on the kill, the devastating strength of a whirlwind, the driving thrust of a torrentially raging river. God alone is able to quell this inner force of hatred. God's transformation of hate into love and forgiveness is what transforms napalm bombs into bags of rice for the hungry and needy of the world.

The scripture gives no alternatives to "love your enemy." There are no qualifications that under certain circumstances this imperative does not apply. It says simply, "Love your enemies." In other words, this *is* a part of the Christian code of behavior. Christians love their enemies.

When we follow Jesus, we will not hate our enemies, for we will have the Spirit's mind. Hence, we will not render pain for pain. We will not consider those who injure us as foes.

Wesley experienced the power of Christ's Spirit to turn hatred into love and forgiveness, as an incident in his *Journal* reveals.

> Mon. October 1st. I expounded Isaiah 35, with great freedom and power. In the hours of the conference, the following persons declared to me their faith in Him who justifies the ungodly!—
>
> Mary Brown, took with strong trembling last night at the Hall, was there set at liberty both from fear and guilt. "I love all . . . ," she said, (the best proof of faith) "and could die for my worst enemy."
>
> —*Journal,* vol. I, p. 183

34

Are We Hard-hearted?

When Pharaoh saw that there was respite, he hardened his heart.

—Exodus 8:15, KJV

How oft have I, like Pharaoh, proved
A penitent in vain,
And when I saw the plague removed
Returned to sin again!
Hardening my heart, I still rebel,
The worse for each reprieve:
But try if grace cannot prevail,
And now, O Lord, forgive.

—*Scripture Hymns* (1762)

The Lord hardened the heart of Pharaoh.

—Exodus 9:12, KJV

There needed, Lord, no act of thine,
If Pharaoh had a heart like mine:
One moment leave me but alone,
And mine, alas, is turned to stone.

Thus if the blessing thou restrain,
The earth is hardened by the rain
Withheld: and thus, if God depart,
Jehovah hardens Pharaoh's heart.

—*Scripture Hymns* (1762)

How can we relate our experience to that of an ancient Egyptian monarch? Wesley simplifies the matter. He internalizes Pharaoh's experience and mirrors his own in it. Therefore, he discovers that the Pharaoh who oppressed the Hebrews is very much up-to-date.

Like Pharaoh, we harden our hearts. Often we are penitent with the hope of relief from evil, difficulty, pain, sickness, or even death. Yet, when relief comes, we are sometimes no longer penitent and forget we have received a reprieve. Perhaps we even take our new lease on life for granted and lapse into the same sinful life we led previously. Worse still, this becomes a pattern of our behavior, and we make our hearts harder each time we repeat it.

> Hardening my heart, I still rebel,
> The worse for each reprieve.

Our hearts are so hard that no action of God is needed to harden them. Wesley gives us a new perspective from which to view the scripture's claim that God hardened Pharaoh's heart. That is not an issue when we acknowledge that, left to our own devices, our hearts are harder than Pharaoh's.

> There needed, Lord, no act of thine,
> If Pharaoh had a heart like mine.

The act of God needed is the divine heart surgery that replaces hearts of stone with hearts of flesh which are alive and beating with God's love.

The prophet Ezekiel gives us hope when he describes such surgery performed by a God who by grace forgives and gives new life. "A new heart I will give you, and a new spirit I will put within you; and I will take out of your flesh the heart of stone and give you a heart of flesh" (Ezekiel 36:26, RSV).

The heart is the central, unifying, life-giving force in us, and God will give it new life. The New Testament describes the experience for followers of Christ in these words:

> Out of his infinite glory, may he give you the power through his Spirit for your hidden self to grow strong, so that Christ may live in your hearts through faith, and then, planted in love and built on love, you will with all the saints have strength to grasp the breadth and the length, the height and the depth; until, knowing the love of Christ, which is beyond all knowledge, you are filled with the utter fullness of God.
>
> —Ephesians 3:16–19, TJB

35

Are We Filled with the Spirit?

Jesus, plant thy Spirit in me;
Then the fruit shall sow the tree,
Every grace its Author prove,
Rising from the root of love.

Joy shall then my heart o'erflow,
Peace which only saints can know,
Peace, the seal of cancelled sin,
Joy, the taste of heaven within.

Gentle then to all and kind
To the wicked and the blind,
Full of tenderness and care,
I shall every burden bear;

Glad the general servant be,
Serve with strict fidelity,
Life itself for them deny,
Meekly in their service die.

—*Scripture Hymns* (1762)

The New Testament parable of the sower stresses the importance of where the seeds are cast, for the nature of the soil on which they fall determines the growth. Wesley speaks in this prayer of the seed of the Spirit which is sown *within us* by Jesus. Our inner being, heart and soul, is the soil. As in the first psalm, people are likened in this poem to fruit-bearing trees.

When the seed of the Spirit has been planted in us by Jesus, the main root of the tree—which becomes the primary source of growth, strength, and food for all the branches—is *love.* It gives life and fruit-bearing ability to the Spirit tree. The Christian is the Spirit tree and bears fruit according to the growth of the power of the Spirit within. The line, "Every grace its Author prove," tells us that a tree's bearing or posture is determined by its roots. If they are shallow and in unfirm ground, the tree may bend over easily or be blown down by the wind. If they are not watered and nourished, and if the surrounding soil is not kept fertile, the tree will wither and die. Every grace which Christians exhibit attests to the Author of their lives, their source of strength and nurture. That is, the bearing of Christians—how people experience their actions and manner of speech—reveals whether or not all the graces in their lives stem from the root of love.

Often you can determine the type of tree by its bearing or posture. The drooping limbs of a weeping willow project a picture of pathos. A giant redwood reigns with regality over the smaller trees of the forest. The sprawling stumps and winding limbs of a cypress tree reflect survival at all costs in water or on land. Likewise you determine whether persons are Spirit trees by their bearing or posture, physically, mentally, spiritually.

Trees are often identified by the fruits they bear. Orange, lemon and apple trees are so called because they bear those fruits. Spirit trees, Christians, are also known by the fruits they bear: gentleness, tenderness, caring, service, joy, peace, faithfulness, meekness. How can others tell if we are Spirit trees? They will know God's Spirit has been planted within us if our hearts overflow with joy; if we personify peace in all that we are; if we are gentle and kind to everyone; if we are tender, loving, and caring and bear the burdens of others; if we happily and faithfully serve God and others; if we live lives of self-denial for the sake of service; and if we live as meek servants all our days.

Are We All Alone?

I, even I only, am left.

—1 Kings 19:10, KJV

Like him in piety's decay
  I made my solitary moan;
Thou heard'st thy desolate servant say,
  I, even I, am left alone!
But now with open heart and eyes
  Thousands I in our Israel see,
Who idols hate, the world despise,
  Its god renounce, and follow thee.

—*Scripture Hymns* (1762)

The agony and pathos conveyed through the musical setting for this verse of scripture in the beautiful aria, "It is enough," in Felix Mendelssohn-Bartholdy's oratorio *Elijah* evoke empathy for this prophet of God. Elijah is weary of his struggle for God against the evil forces and gods of the world. The worshipers of the god Baal have slain other prophets, vandalized God's altars, and want to kill him. Wesley sees Elijah's "solitary moan," however, as a symptom of piety's decay.

We tend to think of Elijah as a giant among the early prophets who performed extraordinary feats demonstrative of great faith. Yet, in the moment of greatest despair, when he prays for his life to be taken away, according to Wesley he suffers from piety's decay. Why? The cry, "I, even I only, am left," is self-centered and reflects the decline in his own faithfulness. Distress and anxiety have blurred his vision.

Like the prophet, Wesley knew what it meant to confront the loneliness of a threatening mob, as he did in England during the 1740s. He was often violently attacked by outraged crowds, for many of the clergy and laity of the Church of England opposed his itinerant preaching and teaching ministry, especially among the Methodist societies. He also knew the peril of self-centered moans of despair in the solitude of ridicule and threats of personal harm and death. Yet, he discovered that it is faith which opens our hearts and eyes to see that we are not alone.

Times will come in the journey of faith when it seems that we stand alone. But if we commit ourselves fully to the hope of faith's promises, the soundness of our fidelity to God and others will not be shaken. Those promises are manifold, but two of the most powerful and sustaining are as follows. First, we are not alone! God is with us! Jesus says, "Lo, I am with you always, to the close of the age" (Matthew 28:20, RSV); "I will not leave you desolate; I will come to you" (John 14:18, RSV). Second, we are not alone! Others are with us! "Since we are surrounded by so great a cloud of witnesses, let us also lay aside every weight, and sin which clings so closely, and let us run with perseverance the race that is set before us" (Hebrew 12:1, RSV).

37

Are We Ministers?

He charged them to tell no one what had happened.

—Luke 8:56, RSV

O may I never take the praise,
  Or my own glory spread,
If made thine instrument to raise
  A sinner from the dead!
O may I never boast my own
  Successful ministry,
But sink forgotten and unknown,
  And swallowed up in thee!

—*Scripture Hymns* (1762)

Charles Wesley records the account of being confronted by a clergyman who complained of George Whitefield's criticism of the clergy in his journal.

> I told him, if he himself was a carnal, worldly-minded Clergyman, I might do what he would call railing,—warn God's people to beware of false prophets. I did not say, because I did not know him, that he *was* one of those shepherds that fed themselves, not the flock; of those dumb dogs that could never have enough: if he was, I was sorry for him, and must leave that sentence of Chrysostom with him, "Hell is paved with the skulls of Christian Priests."
>
> —*Journal,* vol. I, p. 197

Authentic Christian ministry has no room for self-aggrandizement. When greed and success become primary motives for ministry, and obsessions with broadcasting one's success and feeding oneself dominate the goals of ministry, one does nothing more than pave the streets of hell with the skull of another Christian clergyperson.

Authentic Christian ministry has two primary foci which are clearly articulated in Wesley's poem:

1. To bring life where there is death—

> O may I never take the praise,
> Or my own glory spread,
> If made thine *instrument to raise*
> *A sinner from the dead!*

2. To be swallowed up in God—

> O may I never boast my own
> Successful ministry,
> But sink forgotten and unknown,
> And swallowed up in thee!

Recently while reading a newspaper of a major denomination, I came across the "Winners Column," which contained a list of names of clergy and the numbers of persons they had brought into church membership on profession of faith during a specified period of time. While the dissemination of such information may be viewed as encouraging the growth of the church, it is in large measure contrary to the spirit of Jesus' words in Luke 8 and Wesley's understanding of them.

It is inevitable that people will respond to strong ministerial leadership and that churches will grow and thrive when their clergy diligently apply themselves. If, however, one is instrumental in raising a single sinner from death through the gift of life in Christ, it is God alone who is worthy of praise.

Here are some simple rules for ministry which apply to both clergy and laity:

1. In all things give God the glory.
2. Do not spread your personal praise.
3. Do not boast about your successes.
4. Be willing to be forgotten and unknown.

38

How Do We Do God's Will?

Come, let us anew
Our journey pursue,
Roll round with the year,
And never stand still, 'till the Master appear;
His adorable will
Let us gladly fulfill,
And our talents improve
By the patience of hope, and the labor of love.

Our life is a dream,
Our time as a stream
Glides swiftly away,
And the fugitive moment refuses to stay,
The arrow is flown,
The moment is gone,
The millenial year
Rushes on to our view, and eternity's here!

O that each in the day
Of his coming might say
"I have fought my way thro',
"I have finished the work thou didst give me to do!"
O that each from *the* Lord
May receive the glad word,
"Well and faithfully done,
"Enter into my joy, and sit down on my throne!"

—*Hymns for New Year's Day* (1750)

A new year brings with it the hope of beginning again. Resolutions express desires to avoid wrong directions of the past and fulfill new dreams of the future. Just as the early church lived with a sense of urgency and hope of a time fulfilled by the Messiah's return, we, too, live with that hope. It is this sense of urgency that gives us the momentum to pursue our journey anew. It is a messianic hope which sends us out each day. It is the hope of a Messiah who came, comes, and comes again to reconcile broken and divided humankind. Unlike the misguided Thessalonians, who misunderstood Paul's anticipation of the end of the age to mean they should pool their resources and wait for the Messiah's return, we are to be active, not complacent in the time allotted to us.

Two directions for our journey remain constant regardless of how people and the world change with time. First, gladly fulfill God's will. Second, improve our talents. Both of these we do through the patience of hope and the labor of love. In moments of serious doubt and despair it is the patience of hope which gives us the endurance to live with life's circumstances long enough to see the will of God worked out in them. To be sure, we will find it difficult to do God's will or improve our talents through impatience and despair.

Doing God's will and improving talents are accomplished through the labor of love. Love is a labor, not an inactive state. It is something we do! Love is our business. Love is our full-time occupation. When we live out love as Jesus did upon the cross, by giving ourselves for God and others, we are doing God's will. When we love ourselves as God's creation and nourish our talents as God's children, our talents *will* improve. This means that fundamental to doing God's will and improving talents is an active life of love.

Why Is Music Important in Our Lives?

Thou God of harmony and love,
Whose name transports the saints above
  And lulls the ravished spheres,
On thee in feeble strains I call,
And mix my humble voice with all
  Thy heavenly choristers.

If well I know the tuneful art
To captivate an human heart,
  The glory, Lord, be thine.
A servant of thy blessed will
I here devote my utmost skill
  To sound the praise divine.

Suffice for this the season past:
I come, great God, to learn at last
  The lesson of thy grace.
Teach me the new, the gospel song,
And let my hand, my heart, my tongue
  Move only to thy praise.

Thine own musician, Lord, inspire,
And let my consecrated lyre
  Repeat the Psalmist's part;
Thine only Son reveal in me,
And fill with sacred melody
  The fibres of my heart.

So shall I charm the listening throng,
And draw the living stones along
  By Jesus' tuneful name.
The living stones shall dance, shall rise,
And form a city in the skies,
  The new Jerusalem.

O might I with thy saints aspire,
The meanest of that dazzling choir
  Who chant thy praise above!
Mixed with the bright musician band
May I an heavenly harper stand
  And sing the song of love!

—*Redemption Hymns* (1747)

Although Wesley wrote this prayer for musicians before he was married and became a father, he may have prayed it often after his sons, Charles, Jr. and Samuel, demonstrated unusual musical gifts as children and later became distinguished musicians. Letters to them and his wife are filled with admonitions to be faithful in their keyboard practice. Wesley knew that the stewardship of talents, which are God's gifts, is an imperative for the faithful. Therefore, in this poem he writes the Christian artist's manifesto.

I here devote my utmost skill
  To sound the praise divine.

Wesley's poetry and life resound with the spirit of Johann Sebastian Bach's ascription to his compositions: *soli deo gloria* (to God alone be glory).

If well I know the tuneful art
To captivate an human heart,
  The glory, Lord, be thine.

It is a custom in many churches for choir members, organists, and others involved in musical leadership to pray in preparation for worship. Such prayers may be offered by clergy or laity. How appropriate is each of the above selected stanzas for such a purpose! Music is at the heart of worship. When we praise God with music, we blend our strains of exultation with the concert sounds of heaven and earth across the ages which laud the Author of all harmony: God the Creator.

Wesley succinctly stresses the vocational task and theological purpose for the use of music and all other talents:

And let my heart, my hand, my tongue
Move only to thy praise.

Composers, lyricists, arrangers, instrumentalists, and vocalists—all makers of music—are stewards or trustees of the sounds which are the gift of creation. Those sounds which are shaped into what is called music have special qualities which make music important in our lives.

Music teaches (stanza three). Every musician knows the value of sound music lessons and teaching. Even after one no longer studies formally, one should continue to grow, learn, and mature as personal abilities and talents are developed further. Attitudes as well as personal and psychological development are also vital to the musician's learning process. Wesley perceives that one of the most important growth experiences for the musician is "the lesson of grace" taught by the Author of harmony.

Suffice for this the season past:
I come, great God, to learn at last
The lesson of thy grace.

From the lesson of grace we learn that the song of life is God's gift, "the new, the gospel song." It is the song musicians sing, play, compose, and arrange all their lives—"the song of love!" Love alone, as God reveals in the life, death, and resurrection of Jesus, reclaims human life and makes it viable and meaningful. Musicians are involved in giving shape and form to life and its sounds. And if their task is to have meaning, it must be embued with this sense of love.

Music inspires (stanza four). It creates moods. It can make us happy, sad, melancholic, nostalgic, energetic. All about us are examples of the use of music to create atmospheres conducive to productive work, sound mental concentration, body and mind development, and healing. Unquestionably music has great therapeutic value. Consider the ancient example of David's soothing of King Saul's spirit with music from his lyre (1 Samuel 16:23).

In stanza four, musicians pray with Wesley to be inspired by God so that their consecrated talents will "repeat the Psalmist's part." If musicians seek inspiration; if they want their music to be infused with a sense of awe and wonder; if they want to capture the colors and sounds of creation; if they want to catch the spirit of the gospel; if they want to be filled with sacred melody; they should read and sing the Psalms.

Music shapes destiny (stanza five). In this stanza Wesley draws his imagery from First Peter 2:5, "Like living stones be yourselves built into a spiritual house, to be a holy priesthood, to offer spiritual sacrifices acceptable to God through Jesus Christ" (RSV). Music as a part of creation and our lives participates in shaping destiny—in the building of a spiritual house. Hence, musicians and those who listen to their music are the living stones which dance and rise

> And form a city in the skies,
> The new Jerusalem.

That which inspires them and shapes them for their labor is the tuneful name of Jesus. Therefore, the musician's noblest aspiration is to sing the song of love. That is the eternal song the Author of all harmony sings through the life of Jesus.

Music spreads love (stanza six). Musicians who come from different language, cultural, political, social, economic, and religious backgrounds can gather to play a symphony by Beethoven, Mendelssohn, Mahler, or Brahms and suddenly have all their differences be of little or no consequence. What matters is, Can they make harmonious and beautiful music together? This is a parable for musicians as followers of Jesus. What matters most is, Can they sing the song of love harmoniously in concert to the God of Creation and all God's creatures, great and small?

The God of harmony and love of whom Wesley speaks desires that the music of creation resound with harmony and love.

VI

Daily Living

Thanks be to God,
the first thing I felt today
was a fear of pride,
and desire of love.

Charles Wesley

40

What Makes the Impossible Possible for Us?

And these words which I command you this day shall be upon your heart.

—Deuteronomy 6:6, RSV

The table of my heart prepare,
(Such power belongs to thee alone)
And write, O God, thy precepts there,
To shew thou still canst write in stone,
So shall my pure obedience prove
All things are possible to love.[1]

—*Scripture Hymns* (1762)

"These words which I command you this day" (6:6) refer, of course, to the preceding two verses of the chapter. Deuteronomy 6:4 ("Hear, O Israel: the LORD is our God, the LORD alone")[2] is known as the *Shema* in Jewish tradition and is to be repeated twice daily and posted on the entrance to a dwelling. These words are to be at the center of one's being and to accompany one each day and night.

What does the Book of Deuteronomy say to us in these words? It says that God alone is our God. It also says that we are to love God with our whole being. These are the fundamental precepts at the center of our relationship with God. Even if we have hardened hearts, God is able to leave the imprint of these words there. We are not told, "Make God your God, or else!" in a threatening manner. Rather, because God is God we shall love God with all that we are: heart, soul, and strength.

The realization that God is our God alone opens to us the possibilities of love: "All things are possible to love." King David, an adulterer, becomes a writer of eloquent psalms of praise to God. Moses, a murderer, is chosen by God to lead the Hebrew people out of Egyptian bondage. Saul, a persecutor of followers of Jesus, becomes Paul the apostle and author of many New Testament books. With God the impossible becomes possible. We can never know what we might become unless we commit ourselves completely to love God with our whole being.

---

1. The six stanzas examined in the following six meditations are based on Deuteronomy 6:6–7. They originally appeared as one poem in *Scripture Hymns* (1762).
2. Alternate reading in the RSV translation.

41

What Can We Learn?

You shall teach them diligently to your children.

—Deuteronomy 6:7, RSV

Father, instruct my docile heart,
Apt to instruct I then shall be,
I then shall all thy words impart,
And teach (as taught myself by thee)
My children in their earliest days,
To know, and live the life of grace.

—*Scripture Hymns* (1762)

We spend the first years of our lives being taught by others. At the outset we learn essential skills such as walking and talking. As our minds and bodies develop, we begin to appropriate and apply our skills and abilities to a variety of tasks. We learn that they can be used for good and evil. Therefore, what we are taught and by whom determines in large measure the path of life we will pursue in the future.

Reflecting on Deuteronomy 6:7, Wesley says that above all else children should be taught that God is the center of all life and to love God with all that they are. This means that from the earliest age children learn that the main force of their lives, from which the energy and momentum for all they do originates, is God.

The primary responsibility for such instruction lies with the parent. One of the most awesome responsibilities ever entrusted to a human being is to teach a child. This is no doubt why parents and other teachers of children must spend time in private for prayer, meditation, and Bible study in order to receive God's instruction. Paul reminds us of the importance of divine instruction when he says that "the gospel which was preached by me is not man's gospel. For I did not receive it from man, nor was I taught it, but it came through a revelation of Jesus Christ" (Galatians 1:11–12, RSV).

Christian education of children which seeks to impart knowledge *about* God without instructors who constantly seek God's instruction is doomed. Relationships to God are not established by communicating facts and ideas, as important as they may be for the growing dimensions of a relationship to God. Those who would nurture children in a relationship with God must seek first God's nurture of their own lives through a lifelong pattern of behavior which involves prayer, study, self-examination, and acts of faith.

Love is the focus of teaching as understood in Deuteronomy. If instructed in love, if taught to love, if loved by their teachers, children will catch the spirit of love and will learn from their earliest days "to know, and live the life of grace." "The life of grace" is one whose foundation, goal, and purpose is love. This is the heart of Jesus' life, ministry, death, and resurrection. Jesus personified self-giving love. We are to personify it as well.

How Can We Grow?

You shall talk of them when you sit in your house.

—Deuteronomy 6:7, RSV

When quiet in my house I sit,
Thy book be my companion still,
My joy thy sayings to repeat,
Talk o'er the records of thy will,
And search the oracles divine,
'Till every heart-felt word is mine.

—*Scripture Hymns* (1762)

On the evening of March 25, 1736, while in the American colony of Georgia, Charles Wesley recorded in his *Journal:* "After spending an hour at the camp, in singing such Psalms as suited the occasion, I went to bed in the hut, which was thoroughly wet with the day's rain" (vol. I, pp. 10–11). This was almost two years before his conversion experience in May of 1738, although he was already an ordained clergyman of the Church of England. Both before and after his transforming encounter with Christ, Wesley was committed to daily time in quiet meditation and study, whether it be reading the Psalms and lectionary passages appointed by the Church of England for the day or other parts of the Bible.

This stanza of the poem based on Deuteronomy 6:7 provides a simple and helpful design for daily personal growth as a servant of God.

Set aside a quiet time for yourself, God, and the scriptures. Wesley has appropriated "these *words* which I command you," which are to be the object of constant reflection and living, in the larger sense of the entire holy scripture. If we understand that the purpose of the whole Bible is summarized in Deuteronomy 6:4–5 ("Hear, O Israel: The LORD is our God, the LORD alone; and you shall love the LORD your God with all your heart, and with all your soul, and with all your might."), Wesley's appropriation of *these words* as the *Word* is valid and meaningful.

Repeat the sayings of scripture as the source of great joy. Listen to them over and over again. Memorize them and discuss them. They are indeed records of God's will and way with the people of the earth. The more intimate we become with God's will in the lives of sacred history, the better we will understand God's will for our own lives.

Study the scripture in depth. It has been claimed that most of the Bible could be reconstructed from the hymns and poetry of Charles Wesley. This is because he was committed to "search the oracles divine." The recitation, memorization, and reading of God's word takes on its full meaning *only* when we plunge into the depths of each book with the desire that "every heart-felt word" will become a part of our being.

Dietrich Bonhoeffer reminds us how important our immersion in God's word is:

> It is the divine intention that we find God in the entire Bible. That may seem like a very primitive matter. But you have no idea how happy we[1] are, when we find our way back from the dead end streets of some theologies to this primitive matter.[2]

---

1. In the German original, this pronoun and the one following are singular.

2. Dietrich Bonhoeffer, *Gesammelte Schriften,* edited by Eberhard Bethge, vol. III (Munich, 1960), pp. 28, 30.

What Is Most Important?

. . . and when you walk by the way.

—Deuteronomy 6:7, RSV

O might the gracious words divine
Subject of all my converse be,
So would the Lord his follower join,
And walk, and talk himself with me,
So would my heart his presence prove,
And burn with everlasting love.

—*Scripture Hymns* (1762)

Wherever we go, the primary focus of our thought, behavior, and speech should be that God alone is our God and everything about us should express our love for God. This is the spirit of the words in Deuteronomy 6:4–5 and the spirit of the whole of God's word in scripture. It was the force of Charles Wesley's life wherever he went. God was his partner in conversation through the word as his poetry and letters indicate. Although he was often riddled with doubt, no matter where he was or with whom he found himself, Wesley's chief concern was to embody God's presence and be aflame with the divine love he discovered in Jesus Christ. This was his passion, the fire that sparked his vibrant concern for others. It is perhaps nowhere more beautifully expressed than in a letter he wrote to Mr. John Kelway, the distinguished music teacher of his gifted son, Charles, Jr. It was written after they happened to meet, having not seen each other for many years.

November 23, 1776

Dear Sir,

The joy I felt at seeing you on Monday somewhat resembled the joy we shall feel when we meet again without our bodies. Most heartily I do thank God that He has given you a longer continuance among us; and, I trust, a resolution to improve your few last precious moments. *We* must confess, at *our* time of life, that "one thing is needful," even to *get ready for our unchangeable eternal state.* But what is that readiness or meetness?

You are convinced of my sincere love for your soul, and therefore allow me the liberty of a friend. As such I write, not to teach you what you do not know, but to stir up your mind, by way of remembrance, and exhort both you and myself,

> "Of little life the most to make,
> And manage wisely your last stake."

When God came down from heaven to show us the way thither, you remembered his first words: "The Kingdom of God is at hand: *repent* ye, and *believe* the Gospel." He himself declares, "The kingdom of God is within you; even righteousness, and peace, and joy in the Holy Ghost:" and assures us, every one that seeks, finds it; every one that asks, receives it.

"Him hath God exalted, to *give* both repentance and remission of sins:" faith also is the gift of God, through Jesus Christ, its Author and Finisher.

The true repentance is better felt than described. It surely implies a troubled and wounded spirit, a broken and contrite heart. It is what the publican felt when he could only cry, "God be merciful unto me a sinner;" what Peter felt when Jesus turned and *looked* on him; and what the trembling jailer felt when he asked, "What must I do to be saved?"

By this brokenness of heart our Savior prepares us for divine faith and present pardon, sealed upon the heart, in peace which passes all understanding, in joy unspeakable and full of glory, and in love which casts out the love of sin, especially our bosom sin, our ruling passion, whether the love of pleasure, of praise, or of money.

Now, my dear Sir, this meetness for heaven is what I must earnestly wish you and myself, even repentance, faith, and love: and all things are now ready for you. One look of Jesus Christ can break your heart this moment, and bind it up by faith. One day is with Him as a thousand years: and He is still the Man who receiveth sinners; "the same yesterday, today, and for ever."

"I will pardon those whom I reserve," is His own promise; and for this gracious end He has reserved you, and held your soul in life for above seventy years; for this end He has delivered you in innumerable dangers, blessed you with innumerable blessings; and for this end, I humbly hope, His providence brought you acquainted with, dear Sir,

The faithful servant and friend of your soul,

C.W.

—*Journal,* vol. II, pp. 285–6

As this letter indicates, the "gracious words divine" were indeed the subject of Wesley's conversations. There can be no question about the focus of his life: it was on the word of God—whether preaching, teaching, writing letters or poetry, recording experiences in his journal, or casually encountering people in his daily activities.

Let us so sharply focus on God's word that wherever we go, whatever we do, and whomever we encounter, God will be the partner in all our conversation and we shall be aflame with love.

How Do We Prepare for the Evening and Rest?

...and when you lie down.

—Deuteronomy 6:7, RSV

Oft as I lay me down to rest,
O may the reconciling word,
Sweetly compose my weary breast,
While on the bosom of the Lord
I sink in blissful dreams away,
And visions of eternal day.

—*Scripture Hymns* (1762)

In his letters and *Journal,* Charles Wesley often expressed the physical and mental fatigue which pursued him throughout his life. During his itinerant ministry, he traveled hundreds of miles on horseback, preached sometimes more than a dozen times a week, often was attacked by unruly mobs, and was possessed by a daily inner drive to express the breadth and depth of the Christian faith in poetry. After his marriage to Sarah Gwynne at the age of forty-two came the additional responsibilities of husband, father, and parish priest. Charles Wesley was accustomed to lying on his bed to rest with his body fatigued, his composure taxed, his strength spent.

The sixth chapter of Deuteronomy helped him to understand that rest, sleep, and regaining physical and mental composure are a vital part of expressing love for God. Indeed, if we love God with our whole being, replenishing our strength is an essential part of that love and requisite to faith and Christian service.

God's word is the divine prescription for rest.

Oft as I lay me down to rest,
O may the reconciling *word*
Sweetly compose my weary breast.

During the third week of May, 1738, the week of his conversion, Charles Wesley had wrestled with Martin Luther's commentary on the Book of Galatians and yearned to know the God whose love was poured out to him in Jesus Christ. After struggling to grasp such an overwhelming self-giving love, he recorded in his *Journal:*

> I labored, waited, and prayed to feel "who loved *me* and gave himself for *me*." When nature, near exhausted, forced me to bed, I opened the book upon, "For he will finish the work, and cut it short in righteousness, because a short work will the Lord make upon earth." After this comfortable assurance that He would come, and would not tarry, I slept in peace.
>
> —*Journal,* vol. I, p. 88

Wesley followed the divine admonition of Deuteronomy 6:4: When he laid down to rest, he focused his thoughts on God and God's word.

When we live lives of total commitment to God, we prepare ourselves for rest and composure in this way. With God's word in our minds and on our lips and the love of God in our hearts, we can rise refreshed to meet the needs of each new moment.

45

How Do We Prepare for the Day?

. . . and when you rise.

—Deuteronomy 6:7, RSV

Rising to sing my Savior's praise,
  Thee may I publish all day long,
And let thy precious word of grace
  Flow from my heart, and fill my tongue,
Fill all my life with purest love,
And join me to thy church above.

—*Scripture Hymns* (1762)

The all-consuming passion for every day we live is the love of God. According to Deuteronomy, God's love is to pervade all that we are: body, mind, and spirit. Loving God totally is to be the subject of our conversation and action from the time we rise in the morning until we retire in the evening.

Rising to sing my Savior's praise,
Thee may I publish all day long.

As he often does, Wesley moves beyond doctrinal and denominational boundaries in these lines and stresses three essentials for the Christian's daily walk with God. "Thee may I publish all day long" emphasizes that the priority of the glad tidings of the gospel is not a specific set of doctrines, not acceptable formulations of faith language. Rather it is the constant awareness that "God was in Christ, reconciling the world" (2 Cor. 5:19, KJV). Therefore, the word that we have for those about us every day is God's "precious word of grace." In other words, we fill our hearts and tongues with thoughts and words of mercy, healing, compassion, reconciliation, tenderness, justice, goodness, kindness, and love. Finally, it is never enough to have the intent of our hearts right and to speak words embued with God's grace. We must ask God for the supreme gift: "Fill all my life with purest love."

Each morning, inspired by Deuteronomy 6:4–7 as was Wesley, rise and resolve to be the voice of God's praise, the vehicle of God's grace, and the vessel of God's love.

46

How Shall We Spend Our Time?

Where hast thou gleaned to-day?

—Ruth 2:19, KJV

At evening to myself I say,
Soul, where hast thou gleaned today,
Thy labors how bestowed?
What has thou rightly said, or done?
What grace attained, or knowledge won,
In following after God?

—*Scripture Hymns* (1762)

What have our souls gleaned from the day just passed? Have we reaped a harvest of inner spiritual growth today? Where have we been that would make this possible?

Wesley transforms Naomi's question to her daughter-in-law, Ruth, into one of self-examination and introspection, as one reflects upon the day's course of events. Where we have been during the day determines in large measure what we can glean for our souls. Too often we are preoccupied with gleaning only the sustenance for our daily existence, as was the case with Ruth. We go to work to earn enough money to provide food, clothing, and shelter. Our internal sustenance, however, is as important as the external.

Where have we been today? The surroundings and personal associations of the day are vital to the nurture of our inner life. Are the places we have been and those with whom we have associated conducive to spiritual growth? Wesley tells us there are some questions which will help set a daily course for spiritual growth.

How have we expended our energies today? What are our jobs, professions, occupations? Are they honest and just ways to earn a living? How have we spent our energies at our places of work? Have we honored God and others, or have we used others for our own benefit or exploited them? Have we sought to feed our souls in our labors? Whether we are gainfully employed or not, how we spend our time and energy determines whether or not we will grow inwardly. Daily labor is an opportunity to grow spiritually.

What have we said or done today that was right? Speech and actions also influence inner growth. Speaking and acting rightly reflect who we are deep within. Gossip, harsh words, and constant profanity stunt spiritual growth, as do deceptive, belligerent, or self-serving actions. Every wrong word or deed denies the opportunity to grow inwardly.

What grace have we received today as children of God? Grace is like unearned or undeserved food; that is, by the world's standards we deserve that for which we have labored. Giving food to persons in need who have expended no energy to procure or purchase it is grace in action. We grow spiritually by realizing what we receive from God each day and from those who also follow after God: a lifeguard pulls a drowning person out of the water to safety, a fellow traveler returns a purse or wallet inadvertently left on a bus, a police officer stops a speeding driver on a wet and slippery road. God's unconditional love comes to us in many ways. We grow spiritually as we recognize it and thank God for it.

What knowledge have we received in following after God? Our minds have been given to us for growth. If we do not nurture them daily with study and diligence, we will not grow inwardly. Body, mind, and soul make up the total person. If we do not grow in knowledge, we will be incomplete and only part of the person we should be.

My grandfather set a goal for each day to learn one new English word. Imagine how his vocabulary and means of expressing himself expanded over the years. If we consciously seek to follow after God, we will be unending in our quest for knowledge and the expansion of our minds, which are themselves gifts of grace.

Where have our souls been fed today? Where will they be fed tomorrow?

47

Do We Eat for the Right Reasons?

There is death in the pot.

—2 Kings 4:40, KJV

Death in the pot! 'tis always there,
The bane of all our food,
When we partake it without fear
Without an eye to God.

Unless God sanctify the meat
And bless us, from the sky,
Unless we to God's glory eat,
Our souls by eating die.

—*Scripture Hymns* (1762)

According to Second Kings 4:40, when Elisha came to Gilgal there was a famine. So he had a common meal prepared for all present. One of those preparing the pottage unknowingly put shreds of a poisonous gourd into the pot. Elisha had meal added and the pottage was edible. If he had not done so, all who ate might have become ill and died.

A reporter once asked the late United States senator from New York, Jacob Javitts, who suffered from the fatal Lou Gehrig's disease, how he felt about having a terminal illness. He replied, "We're all terminal in this life." How true! The mortal, physical body is temporal. Yet many of us spend our lives trying to preserve it and extend the span of life as long as possible.

Unquestionably, "There is death in the pot." What we eat can kill us. We have come to describe our dietary needs by such words as well-balanced, low-fat, low-sugar, low-sodium and high-fibre. Much of the population has become more nutrition-conscious and knows the meaning of these words. If we eat improperly, we can expect to suffer the consequences eventually. Numerous fatal diseases are known to be related directly to poor eating habits.

Wesley, of course, is speaking of "death in the pot" at another level. He moves beyond the contents of the pottage and sees this story as a parable which views our eating as directly related to our relationship to God. When we partake of earthly sustenance without a constant awareness of the Sustainer of life, God, it is fatal. The attempt to sustain life without its Sustainer is futile.

Paul says that whether we eat or drink it should be done to God's glory (1 Corinthians 10:31). How do we eat to God's glory? By thinking and praying seriously about God's gift(s) of life before, during, and after we eat; by eating with the purpose of sustaining the body, the temple of the Spirit; by being a disciplined eater, not eating merely to satisfy our whims and special tastes; by sharing our food with others, especially the poor and needy; and by fasting, which increases our awareness of how and for what purpose we eat.

We all have eating habits, be they good or bad. Without question there are physical and psychological reasons behind them. If we seek to lead responsible lives before God, we cannot eat thoughtlessly. Our eating habits have a direct bearing on our relationship to God. They communicate to others the quality of that relationship.

Indeed, our mortal bodies are terminal, but the scripture and biblical faith affirm that life is eternal. Therefore, we eat to sustain body and soul. Let us eat then for our sustenance and God's glory.

Why Pray before Eating?

Parent of good, whose plenteous grace
  O'er all thy creatures flows,
Humbly we ask thy power to bless
  The food thy love bestows.

Thy love provides the sober feast;
  A second gift impart;
Give us with joy our food to taste,
  And with a single heart.

Let it for thee new life afford,
  For thee our strength repair,
Blest by thine all-sustaining word,
  And sanctified by prayer.

Thee let us taste, nor toil below
  For perishable meat;
The manna of thy Love bestow,
  Give us thy flesh to eat.

Life of the world our souls to feed,
  Thyself descend from high:
Grant us of thee, the living Bread,
  To eat and never die.

—*Hymns and Sacred Poems* (1739)

The asking of God's blessing in prayer before a meal, often called a "grace" or "blessing," is common practice in most Christian homes. For many it becomes repetitious and routine. Frequently the same prayer is said before every meal, and the habit can become more meaningful than the words uttered. Although some may pray extemporaneous prayers, many of us have the tendency to use the same phrases over and over again. Unquestionably there is no infallible approach to table graces. It is the attitude of prayer and the spirit in which we enter it that is of primary importance.

Wesley's grace reminds us of a number of God's gifts which, when sought in prayer before meals, will imbue the habit of such prayer with inspiration and meaning. These are God's gifts of power, joy, strength, and love.

The primary attitude with which the Christian comes to the meal table is that what is about to be eaten is "the food thy [God's] love bestows."

Before eating, we implore God's power to bless the food. Hence, mealtime is a time for the imparting of God's power. Frequently, meals become perfunctory. We go through the motions whether eating alone or with others. But meals are times of power—God's power, which shrouds us and the food we eat. Furthermore, the entire meal is the time of God's power, not just the grace beforehand.

Before eating, we ask God to give us joy with which to taste our food. Such joy is God's gift. Eating in despair, when angry or upset, is contrary to the Christian attitude toward mealtime. Such experiences are not only spiritually negative but physically as well, for the body's digestive processes are disturbed under such stress. For the Christian, mealtime is a time of joy!

Before eating, we pray for the renewal of strength that we may live as examples of the new life revealed in Christ. Hence, every mealtime is a time of renewal and resurrection. We become God's instruments of renewed strength and new life even as we break bread.

Before eating, we pray for the gift of God's love. The food we eat is perishable, but God's manna of love is eternal. This is why for the Christian every meal is a love feast!

Wesley makes clear that for Christians each meal is a foreshadowing of Holy Communion, which is the meal of meals, feast of feasts. Daily bread is the preparation and sustenance for partaking of the living bread, Jesus Christ, that we may continually sit at his table in this world and the next.

49

Which Is the Most Important Meal?

Author of life divine
  Who hast a table spread,
Furnished with mystic wine
  And everlasting bread,
Preserve the life thyself hast given,
And feed and train us up for heaven.

Our needy souls sustain
  With fresh supplies of love,
Till all thy life we gain,
  And all thy fullness prove;
And, strengthened by thy perfect grace,
Behold, without a veil, thy face.

—*Hymns on the Lord's Supper* (1745)

During his first year at college, Charles Wesley enjoyed himself more than he applied himself, but of his second year he wrote: "I set myself to serious thinking. I went to the weekly sacrament, and persuaded two or three young students to accompany me, and to observe the method of study prescribed by the Statutes of the University." Thus began the Holy Club at Oxford with a strong commitment to study, prayer, and social service, such as visits to prisoners with food for body and spirit. All of these things were intimately related to and grew out of the power for loving service received from the Lord's Supper, Holy Communion. "I went to the weekly sacrament" was the preface to his activity at Oxford and throughout his life.

I remember as a youngster sitting in church and counting the rows of communicants, wondering how long it would take to get them "fed." I was more concerned about the logistics of Holy Communion than its meaning and power. Reaching adulthood, I realized that various branches of Christendom were also preoccupied with the logistics of this sacred meal, though in a different way. Some preferred to receive the elements of bread and wine standing, others kneeling, and many sitting. These particular postures have become fixed in varied traditions with diverse justification. Standing may symbolize the readiness to go into the world in service. Kneeling may signify the humble reception of God's gift(s) as the proper prelude to service. Sitting may focus upon the resolute stillness and quiet reception of God's power to rise anew to faithful service. While such postures may communicate important attitudes which translate into faithful living, it is the power and momentum we receive from the Lord's Supper to be God's faithful servants which is of primary importance.

Holy Communion is the most vital meal of our lives, for in and through it God preserves life, a divine gift. Wesley reminds us that we come to the table to be fed. Proper spiritual growth requires regular nourishment of the Spirit, that is, partaking regularly of food at the Lord's table. We also come to the table to be trained in preparation for this life and the life to come. The Lord's Supper is a training meal of learning and discipline which gives our lives their most meaningful shape, form, and style.

Finally, we come to the table to receive a fresh supply of love. How often Wesley was overcome by the immensity of God's love in the gift of Jesus, whose life, ministry, death, and resurrection were the supreme expression of God's love for all the world.

On May 25, 1738, just two days after he had written his conversion hymn, "Where shall my wondering soul begin?" Wesley wrote in his journal: "In the prayer of consecration [during Holy Communion] I saw, by the eye of faith, or rather, had a glimpse of Christ's broken, mangled body, as taken down from the cross. Still I could not observe the prayer, but only repeat, 'O love, love!' At the same moment I felt great peace and joy" (*Journal*, vol. I, pp. 95–96).

Strengthened by God's grace and empowered by God's love through Christ as experienced in Holy Communion, Wesley was thrust into the world in search of the poor, needy, outcast, wealthy, and noble, for God's love seeks all people.

50

How Do We Wait on God?

Still, for thy loving-kindness, Lord,
I in thy temple wait:
I look to find thee in thy word,
Or at thy table meet.

Here, in thine own appointed ways,
I wait to learn thy will:
Silent I stand before thy face,
And hear thee say, — Be still!

Be still! and know that I am God;—
'Tis all I live to know;
To feel the virtue of thy blood,
And spread its praise below.

I wait my vigor to renew,—
Thine image to retrieve;
The veil of outward things pass through,
And gasp in thee to live.

—*Hymns and Sacred Poems* (1740)

The Christian vocation of waiting upon God is not a purposeless, idle expenditure of time. It involves careful planning and preparation. From his mother, Wesley had learned as a child the value of a method for the living of each day. Hence, time to be still and know that God is God was set apart in his daily schedule. The reason for moments of such stillness and waiting is simple—to renew vigor in the faith. This means becoming more godlike—discovering that God's image in our lives is a reality. It means passing from the outer world to the inner world of who we really are beneath the surface of what others see. When we are still before God we are given the breath of life that sustains us.

One Christmas during the period when our family lived in West Germany, one of our sons returned home from his first semester at an American university. The pastor of the American Protestant Church in Bonn where we resided invited him to talk with the youth of the parish about his university experience. As a counselor of the group, I was privileged to hear his perceptive and wise words on the value of structuring time to wait upon God. He explained that having spent his youth in Germany, he was in a culture-shock tailspin during his first semester. There was only one thing which saved him from emotional shipwreck: a routine which involved waiting upon God. "I went to church every Sunday for worship, even when it seemed I could not possibly grasp its meaning. I read the scripture and prayed daily, although I often did not comprehend their significance. Finally, I attended my classes and did the work prescribed by the professors. These are the only things which held me together and kept me from flipping out," he said.

An occasional unplanned waiting upon God may stimulate our spiritual growth and emotional stability, but we easily can fall prey to the "I don't have time for that" syndrome. Wesley implores us to take time and gives us a prescription for *planned* waiting upon God: (1) attend worship, (2) study the scripture, (3) receive the sacrament of Holy Communion, (4) practice silence, and (5) witness—spread God's praise abroad on earth for redemption through Christ's sacrifice. These are not optional steps to growth in faith. They are requisites for faithful Christian living and communion with God.

The goals we set for ourselves in waiting upon God are crucial to getting the most out of that time. Wesley's poem points out some of the most important ones: (1) to seek God's lovingkindness, (2) to know God's will, (3) to know God is God, (4) to experience personally the meaning of Christ's sacrifice, and (5) to renew one's faith. When we are scurrying about with too much to do, perhaps we will remember Wesley's words. If we follow his prescription for planning our time with God and pursue these goals, Isaiah's promise will be fulfilled in us and for us:

They who wait for the Lord
shall renew their strength,
they shall mount up with wings
like eagles,
they shall run and not be weary,
they shall walk and not faint.

—Isaiah 40:31, RSV

Conclusion

While Charles Wesley's poetry was born in the eighteenth century, it is still up-to-date. To be sure, at times it employs metaphors, similes, figures of speech, modes of expression, and syntax which are somewhat foreign to us today. Yet, he speaks to us in the twentieth century with an authentic message which addresses us where we are and the questions we face personally and corporately in the life of the global church. Why? Because he speaks from the depths of human need: conflict and despair, tensions created by the injustices in society through misuse of wealth and power, and the necessity of personal and social redemption.

The questions Charles Wesley asked about God, Jesus, faith, others, the world, and self are those we are asking today. Indeed, contemporary contexts are often different, but we live as did Charles Wesley amid the tension of the known and the unknown, the revealed and the unrevealed. His inward cry has become our own:

> Come, O thou Traveller unknown,
>   Whom still I hold, but cannot see,
>
> . . . .
>
> Wilt thou not yet to me reveal
>   Thy new, unutterable name?

These brief lines from his poem, "Wrestling Jacob," remind us that we, too, wrestle with the angel. How we long to know the God whom we cannot see! We yearn for revelation that will make the Unknown known. If we endure, Charles Wesley's affirmation from that same poem will become ours:

'Tis Love, 'tis Love! Thou diedst for me,
I hear thy whisper in my heart.
The morning breaks, the shadows flee:
Pure Universal Love thou art.

The Unknown becomes known in Christ Jesus.

Wesley's poetical journey of faith remains fresh and relevant for us because he does not lose sight of the wonder of creation, the Creator, and the created. He is unendingly awestruck by the possibility of God, the incarnation, God's love in Christ and living the reality of that love on earth, and the transformation of human lives through such love. Charles Wesley is unceasingly "lost in wonder, love and praise." In this way he exemplifies an indispensable pattern for the search for God, the pilgrimage of faith, and the living of faith. Live with a sense of wonder, be continually awestruck by creation, the Creator, and the created. Live the love of Christ by being totally filled with that love, which spills over into the lives of all whom we encounter and which goes in search of others at all costs, even death. Finally, live in constant praise of God even when God seems distantly and painfully unknown. Endure! Be "lost in wonder, love and praise." Such a life can face fear, hate, conflict, despair, and violence with confidence and victory, for "perfect love [the love of Christ Jesus] casts out fear" (1 John 4:18, RSV).

Charles Wesley's call to be an evangel for Christ speaks to human need as vitally today as in his own time. In every age, and certainly in ours, there is a need for human transformation. Hardly a poem of Wesley's slipped from his pen without somehow addressing this issue. He spent his life committed to Christ, who can transform lives, turn evil to good, hate to love, brokenness to wholeness, and alienation to reconciliation. Wesley saw people constantly transformed by God's love in Christ. Salvation, redemption, reclaiming of life was and is a reality! His poetry calls us anew to be evangels in a shattered and fragmented world where fear, war, and hatred still wreck lives. We are to be personifiers of what God's love through Christ does: heals, renews, creates new, builds bridges, makes friends of enemies, gives wholeness to broken individuals and a broken world. We are not called merely to be bearers of the good news of the transforming power of Christ's love, that is, to be only *evangelists.* No! Wesley bids us as does the gospel to be *evangels,* persons who embody God's love in all that we are in thought, word, and deed. Evangels live, tell, *and* personify the good news of Christ.

Index of First Lines

Index of Scriptural References

Index of Subjects

Subjects are followed by the first line of the pertinent hymns/poems and page number.

Index of Original Lines

Original lines which appear edited in this volume. The first line of the hymn is followed by the stanza and designated line(s).

Appendix

List of Wesley Sources Used for This Volume

Hymns and Sacred Poems (1739)
Hymns and Sacred Poems (1740)
Hymns and Sacred Poems (1742)
Hymns for Times of Trouble and Persecution (1744)
Hymns on the Lord's Supper (1745)
Nativity Hymns (1745)
Hymns of Petition and Thanksgiving (1746)
Hymns for our Lord's Resurrection (1746)
Redemption Hymns (1747)
Hymns and Sacred Poems (1749)
Hymns for New Year's Day (1750)
Hymns for Intercession for all Mankind (1758)
Short Hymns on Select Passages of the Holy Scriptures, vols. I & II (1762); references to this work are cited as *Scripture Hymns.*
Manuacript Acts (1764–65[?])
Wesley was definitely writing these poems during 1764, but the actual beginning and concluding dates for the manuscript are confused by his own notation which records the manuscript as begun on "N(ov). 13, 1764" and "Finished, April 24, 1764."
Wesley, Charles. *Journal,* vols. I & II, edited by T. Jackson (London: Mason, 1849).

Dr. Kimbrough is known as author and scholar by his legal name, "S T," as professional singer and musician by the name of "Steven." Over the last two decades he has carved out niches as author, Old Testament specialist, theologian, church musician, professional singer, and actor. He has taught on major university and graduate faculties in the USA and abroad, such as, Princeton Theological Seminary and Bonn University (West Germany). In addition, he has performed on leading concert, musical, and operatic stages around the world: New York, San Francisco, Cincinnati, London, Berlin, Hamburg, Rio de Janeiro, Barcelona, Torino. A graduate of Birmingham Southern College and Duke University Divinity School, he holds a Ph.D. from Princeton Theological Seminary and has published two books: *Israelite Religion in Sociological Perspective* and *The Old Testament as the Book of Christ* (English translation) and numerous articles on biblical, theological, liturgical, and musical subjects.

Dr. Kimbrough's interest in rediscovering the past to enrich the present and future, as in the case of Charles Wesley's eighteenth century poetry, is linked to his study of archeology in Italy, Greece, Jordan, and Israel and to his musical career as well. For example, he has been a major force in rediscovering forgotten European song literature through his many recordings of the art songs of the composers Schreker, Zemlinsky, Korngold, and Weill who were effaced by Nazism's Third Reich. He has recorded a commemorative collection of the *Hymns of Charles Wesley,* and he has also written a musical about Charles Wesley entitled, *Sweet Singer,* which he performed at New York's Carnegie Hall in 1984.

A member of the North Alabama Conference of The United Methodist Church, Dr. Kimbrough serves as a member of the Wesley Consultation and the Psalms Text Committee for the revision of the United Methodist Church hymn and worship book. In 1985 he became a member of the Center of Theological Inquiry, a research institution in Princeton, New Jersey, where he is coediting with Dr. Oliver Beckerlegge the unpublished poetry of Charles Wesley for publication.